Writing Canadian English

Intermediate Student Workbook

Second Edition – Revised

Sheridan Anderson and Karen Roth

Detselig Enterprises Ltd.

Calgary, Alberta, Canada

Writing Canadian English: Intermediate Student Workbook
© 1999 Detselig Enterprises Ltd.

Canadian Cataloguing in Publication Data

Anderson, Sheridan, 1932-
Writing Canadian English: intermediate. Student workbook.

ISBN 1-55059-184-3

1. English language—Textbooks for second language learners.* 2. English language—Grammar—Problems, exercises, etc. 3. English language—Composition and exercises. I. Roth, Karen. II. Title.

PE1128.A544   1999   428.2'4   C99-910186-2

Detselig Enterprises Ltd.
210-1220 Kensington Rd. N.W.
Calgary, Alberta T2N 3P5
www.temerondetselig.com
e-mail: temeron@telusplanet.net
telephone: (403) 283-0900/fax: (403) 283-6947

Detselig Enterprises Ltd. appreciates the financial support received for our 1999 publishing program, provided by Canadian Heritage and other sources.

Printed in Canada.

ISBN 1-55059-184-3

SAN 115-0324

Cover design by Dean Macdonald

Contents

Unit I

Review

Section I: Present Tense, Present Progressive, Tag Endings, Subject/Object/Possessive Pronouns and Possessive Adjectives

A. Rewrite each sentence in the third person singular.

1. I hope I see Mary. _____

2. They go to the movies on weekends. _____

3. We like to skate in winter. _____

4. Bakers bake bread. _____

5. They study hard. _____

6. You do exercises every morning. _____

7. We need a new house. _____

8. Children play a lot. _____

9. Women live longer than men. _____

10. Joe and Jack live in Calgary. _____

B. Rewrite in the negative.

1. The dog likes to run. _____

2. Dentists fix teeth. _____

3. The bus leaves at 6:00 tonight. _____

4. We like to drink tea. _____

5. You can buy clothes in a department store. _____

_____

6. That man builds houses. _____

7. You and I wash the clothes on Mondays. _____

_____

8. Students like to do homework. _____

9. It snows in winter in Vancouver. _____

C. Make questions as in the example. Use the subject suggested in brackets ().

Example: Mary studies English. (you)
Do you study English, too?

1. John drives a car to school. (Marilyn) _____

_____

2. Mrs. Glazer teaches French. (Miss Bell) _____

_____

3. We like to sing. (you) _____

4. They want to eat dinner. (she)_____

5. Diane studies mathematics. (Yoko) _____

_____

6. You have a bicycle. (Bob)_____

7. Mail carriers deliver letters. (police officers) _____

_____

8. I have a dog. (Mary and George) _____

_____

9. Susan stays in bed until noon every day. (Elaine) _____

_____

10. The old people know the story. (young people) _____

_____

D. Use action verbs to make general statements about the following subjects.
Example: Horses run.

1. Doctors_____   6. Fish _____

2. A secretary _____   7. A king _____

3. Children_____   8. Cats don't_____

4. Women _____   9. Students_____

5. Teachers _____   10. A vegetarian doesn't _____

E. Put the verbs in brackets into the present progressive tense.

1. The Prime Minister not (make) a speech on Friday. _____

_____

2. The flowers (bloom) now._____

3. She (write) a book about monkeys. _____

_____

4. You (read) the newspaper now?_____

5. They (stay) at the Banff Springs Hotel. _____

_____

6. I (go) crazy. _____

7. Mary (put) her coat on. _____

8. I not (worry) about that. _____

9. Sherry (wear) a new dress today? _____

_____

10. We (try) to complete the lesson. _____

_____

F. Use the following subjects and verbs to make sentences about things or people that are changing gradually.

Subject (Verb)

1. The old man (go blind) _____

2. Mr. Smith (go bald) _____

3. I (lose weight) _____

4. She (get fat) _____

5. My health (improve) _____

6. His hair (turn grey) _____

7. It (get colder) _____

8. We (not grow old gracefully) _____

9. They (learn to read) _____

10. She (grow taller) _____

G. Fill in the blanks using either the simple present or the present progressive.

1. (read) _____ John _____ now?

2. (write) _____ you always _____ such long letters?

3. (wake) _____ he _____ you every morning?

4. (talk) _____ you usually _____ so much?

5. (study) _____ they _____ in the library at present?

6. (eat) They _____ at eight each day.

7. (have) _____ Jim _____ a shower later this morning?

8. (owe) _____ they _____ you any money now?

9. (play) I _____ tennis on weekends.

10. (love) I _____ my family very much.

H. Rewrite each sentence putting the verb in the simple present or present progressive. Make questions or negatives as required.

1. Where is Elizabeth? She (take) a shower. _____
   _____

2. The boy usually (play) soccer but today he (play) hockey. _____
   _____

3. I always (go) to the movies on the weekends but I never (buy) popcorn._____
   _____

4. You (love) him? No, I (like) him a lot but I (not love) him. _____
   _____

5. The water (boil) now. You (want) a cup of tea? _____
   _____

6. You (look for) Brenda? She (drink) coffee in the cafeteria. _____
   _____

7. The food (smell) so good, I (want) something to eat right now. _____
   _____

8. She (see) another doctor because she (not like) the first one._____
   _____

9. I (write) my paper tonight. _____

10. You (study) English at Mount Royal? _____
    _____

11. Fish (cost) a lot these days. The price (include) a tax?_____
    _____

12. You (have) a driver's license? No, but I (have) my test soon. _____
    _____

13. What your mother (do) now? She (clean) the house. _____
    _____

14. I usually (take) my vacation on Vancouver Island._____
    _____

15. He (not work). He (lie) in the sun._____
    _____

16. It (rain)? No, the sun (shine) and the birds (sing). _____
    _____

17. You (do) anything tonight? Yes, I (go) to a movie._____
    _____

18. What you (eat)? I (eat) a banana because I (like) fruit. _____
    _____

19. What you (wear) today?_____

20. Elaine (jog) every day. She (exercise) also? _____

_____

I. Add the appropriate tag ending.

Example: *I swim, don't I?*
I am swimming, aren't I?

1. You read a lot, _____?
2. You're eating a lot of oranges, _____?
3. He wears pyjamas, _____?
4. She's having a baby,_____?
5. I'm getting taller, _____?
6. Anna isn't listening to the stereo,_____?
7. The children brush their teeth, _____?
8. You don't speak Spanish, _____?
9. The moon shines every night, _____?
10. It's getting warmer, _____?

J. Choose the correct pronoun (either subject or object) to fill in the blanks below. Make it refer to the underlined words in each sentence.

1. The Andersons have a big dog. My friend is afraid to give _____ a cat.
2. Does Mary speak English? _____ appears to understand it well.
3. This is Karen. Please introduce _____ to the other students.
4. The book isn't here. _____ is still in the library.
5. All the teachers want a vacation. _____ think _____ deserve one.
6. Fish is so expensive we don't buy _____ very often.
7. Mr. and Mrs. Daum are visiting us today. Do you know _____ ?
8. Carolyn has a little girl. She loves _____ very much.
9. You and David study hard. Does your teacher give _____ good grades?
10. I want another cup of coffee. Please buy _____ one.

K. Rewrite each sentence changing the underlined words to pronouns.

1. Sherry knows Lorna and Elaine. _____

2. All you students work very hard for your grades. _____

_____

3. The women don't look after their children. _____

4. You and I are going to have a talk with Mary and Joe. _____

_____

5. The dinner is cooking now. I hope the dinner tastes good. _____

_____

L. Make one sentence in the present progressive tense out of each set of words. If possible make a second sentence by changing the order of the direct and indirect objects.

1. The teacher give a test   us.

_____

_____

2. Jim   write a letter   his mother.

_____

_____

3. We   tell   a story   them.

_____

_____

4. The doctor write a prescription me.

_____

_____

5. I   teach it   you.

_____

_____

M. Fill in the blanks with a possessive pronoun or adjective. Make it refer to the underlined words.

1. She thinks she found _____ book.
2. I rode _____ new bicycle yesterday.
3. They never write to _____ parents.
4. David likes _____ job.
5. Look at that dog chasing _____ tail!
6. I'm look for _____ coat. Did you find _____ ?
7. Mary and Jean are doing _____ homework.
8. Andrew and I want to begin _____ work.
9. Our country needs to develop _____ resources.
10. I like _____ class but those Canadian girls don't like _____ .

N. Rewrite the sentences as in the following example.

Example: *The book belongs to John.*
     It is John's book. It is John's.

1. The car belongs to Jim. _____

2. The television belongs to them. _____

_____

3. The beautiful clothes belong to us. _____

_____

4. That horse belongs to Mai. _____

5. The papers belong to you and me. _____

_____

6. The house belongs to you and John. _____

_____

Section II: Simple Past, Tag Endings, Question Words, Prepositions, Reflexive Pronouns

A. Rewrite each sentence changing the verb from the simple present to the simple past.

1. I swim every day. _____

2. We like to play in the park. _____

3. It often snows in Calgary. _____

4. We go skiing at Lake Louise in winter. _____

_____

5. You always try to study hard. _____

6. Mary offers the cake to the children. _____

_____

7. He prefers to drive fast. _____

8. We study English very hard. _____

B. Fill in the blanks with a verb in the past tense.

1. I usually sleep until 8:00 but yesterday I _____ until nine.

2. Tony often wears a tie. He _____ one again yesterday.

3. We generally sit in the front row but last time we _____ in the back.

4. The wind blows hard in the mountains, and last Sunday it _____ very hard.

5. I usually go to the college at 1:00 but yesterday I _____ at 3:00.

6. My brother wins a lot of ski races. Last week he _____ again.

7. People usually stand when the national anthem is sung. Yesterday, we _____ to sing *O Canada* at school.

8. He keeps all his old clothes and last year he _____ his old shoes too.

9. I feel much better today than I _____ yesterday.

10. John likes to draw. Last week he _____ a picture of the teacher.

C. Answer each question using the word in brackets in your answer.
   Example: Did you go home? (school) No, I went to school.

1. Did you learn English in school? (French) _____

2. Did you feel sick? (well) _____

3. Did he sell the Pontiac? (Chevrolet) _____

4. Did you forget the oranges? (apples) _____

5. Did she read the book yesterday? (last week) _____
_____

6. Did they use the bicycles? (car) _____

7. Did the house cost a lot? (a little) _____

8. Did it snow in Lethbridge? (rain) _____

9. Did the restaurant open at 7:00? (6:00) _____

10. Did your parents meet the teacher? (the principal) _____
_____

11. Did that man build the house? (that woman) _____
_____

12. Did you shut the window? (door)_____

D. Make each statement into a question.

1. He became Prime Minister last year._____
_____

2. She broke the plate. _____

3. We chose another dog. _____

4. The clothes cost $100. _____

5. I did my homework last night._____
_____

6. He cut his finger._____

7. She broke her arm. _____

8. Mary dealt the cards. _____

E. Make each statement negative.

1. The children drank a lot of milk._____
_____

2. The bird fell out of the nest. _____
_____

3. I gave her a present._____

4. He hung the picture on the wall._____
_____

5. I heard something outside. _____

F. Rewrite the paragraph to show that the action occurred in the past.

Every day I get up at 7:00. Then I wash, brush my hair and have breakfast. After breakfast I brush my teeth. At 8:00 it is time to leave for work, so I walk to the bus stop and wait for the bus. I arrive at work at 9:00 and stay there until noon. I usually eat lunch in a restaurant and return to work at 1:00. After lunch I work until 5:00 when I take the bus home again.

Twice a week I attend an English class. This begins at 7:30 and lasts until 9:30. At 9:30 we are all tired. We learn about Canada, and we learn many new words and some new grammar each time. I usually get a ride home with a friend in the class. Before I go to bed, I try to do my homework. I am generally asleep by 11:00.

_____
_____
_____
_____
_____
_____
_____
_____
_____
_____
_____
_____

G. Write a paragraph describing what you did yesterday.

_____
_____
_____
_____
_____
_____
_____
_____
_____
_____
_____

H. Add the tag endings to the following sentences.

1. Those were nice shoes,_____?

2. He did his homework, _____?

3. These carrots taste good,_____?

4. She spoke French,_____?

5. That child didn't need his pen, _____?

I. Make questions replacing the underlined words with a question word.

Example: She *wrote the book.* Who *wrote the book?*

1. The dog ate the bone. _____

2. The dog ate the bone. _____

3. The dog ate the bone. _____

4. The old one is mine. _____

5. They met at the movie theatre. _____

6. We were late because the car broke down. _____

7. She waited for three hours. _____

8. He exercises every day. _____

9. It's 5:00 p.m. _____

10. That's John's book. _____

J. Make questions for these answers.

1. The Andersons went to London last year.

When _____

Who _____

Where _____

2. Jim is going to the library to read a book.

Who _____

Where _____

Why _____

What _____

3. I like the new dress better than the old one.

Which_____

Who _____

What _____

4. I put John's coat in the closet.

Who _____

Whose _____

What _____

Where _____

5. Mary wants to borrow John's book because she has lost hers.

Who _____

Whose _____

What _____

Why _____

6. Allan's brother lived in Ontario until he was ten years old. (who, where, how long, whose)

_____

_____

_____

_____

7. John wrote a story about Canadians last year. (what, who, when)

_____

_____

_____

K. Fill in the blanks with the appropriate preposition.

1. They live _____ Woodland Drive.

2. The students complained _____ the test.

3. Her birthday is _____ July 22nd.

4. We read our books _____ the afternoon.

5. Anna usually goes to bed _____ 9:00 _____ night and gets up _____ 8:00 _____ the morning.

6. Last night we went _____ the movie.

7. He's staying _____ the hotel.

8. My sweater is _____ the cleaner's.

9. I live _____ the park.

10. Put the sheets _____ the bed.

11. Please see who is _____ the door.

12. I heard someone _____ the next room.

13. The plane flew _____ the Atlantic.

14. The swimmer dived _____ the water.

15. They take their vacation _____ the mountains _____ the winter.

16. I was born _____ the spring _____ April 2nd.

17. They lived _____ Alberta, _____ Canada.

18. They moved _____ Tokyo, _____ Japan.

19. The student lives _____ 222 Airport Way.

20. Park the car _____ the driveway.

21. Is the book _____ the shelf or _____ the desk? I think it's _____ the drawer.

22. Where can I find the bus _____ Edmonton?

L. Answer each question in the <u>negative</u> including a reflexive pronoun in the answer.

1. Do you study with your friend? _____

2. Do you help your mother with the cooking? _____

_____

3. Is Henry going to the concert with us? _____

_____

4. Are you going to Banff in our car? _____

_____

5. Do you give him the money to buy his books? _____

_____

6. Is the real estate agent helping them find an apartment? _____

_____

7. Does your brother eat with you at night? _____

8. Do you need any help with the luggage? _____

_____

9. Do you watch television with your husband? _____

_____

10. Do you want me to help your parents with the painting? _____

_____

Section III: Future, Tag Endings, <u>Some</u>/<u>Any</u>, Articles, Comparisons, Superlatives of adjectives and adverbs.

A. Put the following sentences in the future tense using <u>will</u>.

1. Do you think he (know) the answer in a few days?_____

_____

2. I'm sure John (lend) you his car. _____

_____

3. You (have) time to help me this afternoon? _____

_____

4. I hope I (find) it soon. _____

5. If you're going to France, you (need) a passport._____

_____

6. It (matter) if I do my homework tomorrow? _____

_____

7. Do you think that she (notice) me?_____

_____

8. If you take that course you (get) a better job._____

_____

B. Put the following sentences into the future tense using <u>going to</u> or <u>will</u>. Make questions or negatives as required.

1. I'm getting fat. I (go) on a diet. _____

_____

2. There's the telephone. Oh, I (answer) it._____

_____

3. You (clean) the house? Yes, you (help) me? _____

_____

4. When you go to the United States you (send) me a postcard? _____

_____

5. Mr. Daum (have) a wine and cheese party next week. _____

_____

6. If you drive too fast you (get) a ticket. _____

_____

7. You (buy) stamps at the Post Office? Yes, I am. Then you (buy) some for me, please? _____

_____

_____

8. You (have) a cup of tea?_____

9. You (leave) those boxes in the doorway? Someone (trip) over them if you do. _____

_____

_____

10. I don't like this book. I not (finish) it. _____

_____

11. This light bulb has burned out. Oh! I (go) and get another one. _____

_____

C. Add the tag endings to the following sentences.

1. You'll buy the tickets, _____ ?
2. They aren't going to miss the test, _____ ?
3. She won't take a vacation this year,_____ ?
4. I'm going to grow tall, _____ ?
5. He'll have a shower, _____ ?

D. Below is a list of nouns. Some of them are count nouns and some are non-count. Put <u>some</u> before the non-count nouns and <u>a/an</u> before the count nouns.

1.	_____ apple	11.	_____ furniture	21.	_____ ink		
2.	_____ coffee	12.	_____ flower	22.	_____ pencil		
3.	_____ electricity	13.	_____ flour	23.	_____ chalk		
4.	_____ fish	14.	_____ sugar	24.	_____ radio		
5.	_____ fruit	15.	_____ rice	25.	_____ butter		
6.	_____ orange	16.	_____ bag	26.	_____ bread		
7.	_____ bone	17.	_____ baggage	27.	_____ vegetable		
8.	_____ blood	18.	_____ transportation	28.	_____ army		
9.	_____ bicycle	19.	_____ car	29.	_____ water		
10.	_____ chair	20.	_____ pen	30.	_____ breath		

E. **Only one of the two nouns given at the left of each sentence can be used in the blank at the right. Choose the correct noun in each case.**

> *Example:* *money, friends*   *Helen has several* <u>*friends*</u>*.*
> *rice, apple*   *Please give me a pound of* <u>*rice*</u>*.*

1. water, glass Mary has a _____.
2. car, travel They want another _____.
3. cup, milk I want some _____.
4. shower, soap He needs some _____.
5. furniture, table Does she have a _____.
6. pencil, chalk She needs some _____.
7. pens, ink The teacher brought several _____.
8. meal, fruit Would you like a _____.
9. fruit, orange Help yourself to some _____.
10. tea, cup of coffee Do you want some _____.
11. rice, beans Does he grow much _____.
12. patience, problem My friend has a lot of _____.
13. news, story Let's listen to a _____.
14. noise, sounds The engine doesn't make much _____.
15. mail, letters There's only a little _____ today.
16. meat, potatoes Please take a few _____.
17. heroes, courage It takes a great many _____ to fight a battle.
18. fog, clouds There is a good deal of _____.
19. friend, groups A _____ came to visit.
20. apple, rice He would like another _____.
21. pennies, money Does he have much _____.
22. information, facts He gave us a few _____.
23. school, classes The children attended some _____.
24. energy, exercise The boy has a lot of _____.
25. clothes, clothing Do you have many _____.
26. chair, furniture I want to buy some _____.
27. baggage, cases They brought several _____.
28. glass, glasses We broke a great deal of _____.
29. car, travel They need a new _____.
30. courage, suggestions Do you have any _____?

F. Insert <u>a</u> or <u>an</u> in the blanks, if necessary.

1. Many people in Canada live in ____ house or ____ apartment.
2. Each house has ____ yard with ____ flowers and ____ trees.

3. Every house has _____ living room, one or two _____ bedrooms, _____ bathroom and _____ kitchen. Some have _____ basements too.

4. In _____ bedroom there is usually _____ bed, and sometimes there is _____ closet, too.

5. _____ people like to sing and dance.

6. _____ men and _____ women like to have _____ nice home.

7. When I stand on _____ corner of _____ street I enjoy watching _____ buses go by.

8. Would you like _____ milk in your tea? No thanks, I just want _____ sugar.

9. I'm going to Europe by _____ plane but on _____ route we must stop in _____ Toronto to pick up _____ passengers.

10. I want to lose _____ weight so I'm going on _____ diet.

G. Insert <u>the</u> in the blanks if necessary.

1. _____ Canada is in _____ continent of _____ North America.

2. _____ French is spoken in _____ France.

3. I teach _____ English language.

4. _____ busiest night of _____ week is always Saturday.

5. I went to see _____ best movie of _____ year.

6. _____ dogs like _____ bones.

7. _____ people of Spain speak _____ Spanish.

8. _____ capital of _____ Canada is _____ Ottawa.

9. He plays _____ soccer for _____ Winnipeg Soccer Team.

10. He's _____ best player on _____ team.

H. Fill in the blanks with <u>a</u>, <u>an</u> or <u>the</u>, if necessary.

1. I can see _____ green trees. They are _____ green because they are covered with _____ leaves. _____ pine trees do not have _____ leaves because they have _____ needles. They also have _____ cones.

2. _____ oranges, _____ lemons and _____ grapefruit are _____ citrus fruits. They all have _____ peel on them which you cannot eat. _____ citrus fruit grows in countries with _____ warm climate.

3. Canada's smallest _____ province is _____ Prince Edward Island. It is located in _____ eastern part of _____ country.

4. I can speak _____ French and _____ English. I think _____ sounds of _____ French are _____ prettier than _____ sounds of _____ English.

5. _____ summer comes to _____ Yukon once _____ year.

6. In _____ school zone you must drive _____ slowly.

7. In general, you drive at _____ 50 kilometres _____ hour, but on _____ highway you can drive at 100 kilometres _____ hour.

8. Tonight I think I'll go to _____ movies. There is _____ good show on at _____ theatre down _____ street.

9. He is going to finish his _____ homework on _____ weekend.

10. If you study _____ lesson hard, you will pass _____ exam next _____ Monday.

I. Make comparisons with <u>as . . . as.</u>

1. John is (tall) Tony. _____

2. I am (busy) she is. _____

3. The cat is (lazy) the dog. _____

4. Marie is (lovely) Jeanette. _____

5. This lesson is (easy) the last one. _____

_____

J. Make comparisons with the adjectives and adverbs given.

Example: *He (short) Mary.*
He is shorter than Mary.

1. You work (hard) I do. _____

2. My parents get up (early) my brother does. _____

_____

3. Kamloops is (near) to Calgary Vancouver. _____

_____

4. He is (happy) she is. _____

5. This course is (difficult) that one. _____

_____

6. I come to class (early) the teacher. _____

_____

7. That dress is (colorful) mine. _____

_____

8. A rose is (lovely) a weed. _____

_____

9. This towel is (dry) yours is. _____

_____

K. Use the superlative form of the adjective or adverb given.

Example: *He works (hard).*
He works the hardest of all.

1. This car is (fast). _____

2. He is a (serious) student. _____

3. You write (good) stories. _____

4. She eats (little). _____

5. Montreal has (many) people. _____

6. This climate is (healthy). _____

7. That child is (happy) in the room._____
_____

8. The Rockies have (beautiful) scenery in Canada._____
_____

L. Answer the questions.

1. Which is the shortest day of the year?_____

2. Who is the best student in the class?_____

3. Who is the nicest person you know?_____

4. Are the wealthiest people the happiest? _____

5. Where is the most beautiful scenery in the world?_____

6. Which country do you like best? _____

7. Which is the most powerful country in the world? _____

8. What are the best conditions for studying? _____

9. Where is the longest river in the world? _____

M. Make one sentence giving the information in the two sentences below.

Example: Peter is twelve. Corri is thirteen. Peter is younger than Corri.

1. That picture is pretty. This picture is ugly. _____
_____

2. I have $100. My brother has $50. _____
_____

3. Gail has two sisters. I have one sister. _____
_____

4. His neighborhood is poor. My neighborhood is also poor. _____
_____

5. He weighs 70 kg. His friend weighs 75 kg._____
_____

6. The hill is high. The mountain is higher. _____
_____

7. I make a lot of mistakes. You make no mistakes._____
_____

Unit II

Present Perfect

A. Change each sentence to (a) negative, (b) interrogative. Use contractions where possible and make any other necessary changes.

Example: *He has opened a savings account.*
(a) *He hasn't opened a savings account.*
(b) *Has he opened a savings account?*

1. I have already saved $100.

(a) _____

(b) _____

2. They have known the bank manager for a long time.

(a) _____

(b) _____

3. The teller has called me to the window to give me my cheques.

(a) _____

(b) _____

4. We have deposited some money in the account.

(a) _____

(b) _____

5. She has paid her utility bills at the bank.

(a) _____

(b) _____

6. You have used up all your cheques.

(a) _____

(b) _____

7. They have had a mortgage on their house for ten years.

(a) _____

(b) _____

8. The bank has given me a loan (in order) to buy a car.

(a) _____

(b) _____

9. He has obtained a credit card from his bank.

(a) _____

(b) _____

10. The bank manager has helped him to budget his money.

(a) _____

(b) _____

B. Fill in the blanks with the correct form of the verb in brackets.

Example: I _____ (invest) my money all my life.
I have invested my money all my life.

1. I _____ (just open) up a savings account.

2. He _____ (have) a chequing account for the last three years.

3. What kind of account _____ you _____ (open)?

4. I _____ (borrow) money from the bank before.

5. How much interest _____ they _____ (charge) you?

6. He _____ (talk) to the bank manager several times.

7. What _____ he _____ (see) him about?

8. We _____ (ask) twice for a loan but we (not receive) _____ one yet.

9. He _____ (make) and _____ (lose) several fortunes.

10. Banking _____ (be) an important part of the life of most Canadians.

11. In addition, trust companies and credit unions _____ (offer) useful services for many years.

12. Some of these services _____ (be) savings accounts and chequing accounts.

13. Banks _____ (offer) the protection of safety deposit boxes as well.

14. Traditionally, banks _____ (provide) help for loans and mortgages.

15. Also, the Canadian people often _____ (find) help with their budgeting problems from the banks.

16. When Canadians _____ (have) the need to use the services of a bank, they always _____ (find) it useful to compare one bank with another as the services and benefits always _____ (vary) greatly.

17. A chequing account _____ (enable) them to pay for things without carrying cash.

18. Most people in the past _____ (open) both a chequing and a savings account.

19. A savings account _____ (help) people accumulate money in a safe and secure manner.

20. In the past, the Government _____ (guarantee) money in the bank up to $60,000.

C. Put the verb in brackets in the present perfect or simple past tense.

Example: I _____ (see) this cheque before. I _____ (see) it last week.
I have seen this cheque before. I saw it last week.

1. People who _____ (want) to save money _____ (be able) to open savings accounts ever since our banking system _____ (begin).

2. If a Canadian _____ (have) a savings account for a year, then she _____ (be able) to receive interest on her money.

3. The bank _____ (give) this interest because for the past year the bank itself _____ (be able) to use the money.

4. If you just _____ (open) a chequing account, the bank probably just _____ (give) you a cheque book too.

5. _____ you (need) to show identification when you _____ (cash) your last cheque?

6. The bank _____ (help) the Andersons to buy their new car last year. They _____ (drive) it 20,000 kilometres since then.

7. The bank _____ (help) me financially for many years.

8. The bank _____ (help) me to remodel my house in 1982.

9. Whenever I _____ (need) credit, I _____ always (go) to the bank which _____ always (help) me.

D. Answer the questions in the (a) affirmative, (b) negative.

Example: *Have you been to the Credit Union yet?*
(a) Yes, I have already been to the Credit Union.
(b) No, I haven't been to the Credit Union yet.

1. Have you applied for a credit card yet?

(a) _____

(b) _____

2. Has the bank approved your mortgage yet?

(a) _____

(b) _____

3. Have they received the cheque yet?

(a) _____

(b) _____

4. Have I paid the bill yet?

(a) _____

(b) _____

5. Have you ever had a term deposit account?

(a) _____

(b) _____

E. Change each phrase using <u>for</u> into one using <u>since</u>. Make other changes if necessary.

Example: *I have worked in the bank for seven days.*
I have worked in the bank since Monday.

1. I have had an account with the Trust Company for ten years. _____

2. He has had a VISA card for a week._____

_____

3. The interest rate has been 13% for the last year._____

_____

4. She has worked as a bank teller for a month. _____

_____

F. Put the verb in brackets into the present perfect or past tense. Use short answers where possible. Be prepared to explain your choice of tense.

Example: Have you heard what the interest rate is?
Yes, I _____ . I _____ (hear) it yesterday.
Yes, I have. I heard it yesterday.

1. Have you put you money in an account yet?
   Yes, I _____ . I _____ (put) it there yesterday.

2. Have you been to the bank yet today?
   No, I _____ . I _____ (go) there yesterday.

3. Has she already written a cheque for the groceries?
   Yes, she _____ . She _____ (write) it straight away.

4. Has he been able to save any money yet?
   Yes, he _____ . He _____ (be able to) save $300 already.

5. Has he charged you any interest yet for the loan?
   Yes, he _____ . He _____ (charge) me 15%.

G. Some of the sentences below are correct, some are not. Put an X beside the wrong ones and rewrite them correctly.

1. Have you been to the bank recently?_____

_____

2. The children have opened a savings account last week. _____

_____

3. I have applied for a credit card a week ago. _____

_____

4. Have you had a bank loan when you were at university?_____

_____

5. I have drawn all my money out of my account last week._____

_____

6. My uncle has written a will and left it in his safety deposit box before he died._____

_____

7. The bank has closed ten minutes ago. _____

8. Have you ever worked as a cashier?_____

9. Has this bank been insured by the Government?_____

_____

10. She has left her jewellery in the bank for safe-keeping until she came back. _____

_____

11. We have bought traveller's cheques before we went on vacation. _____

_____

12. I didn't see the bank manager yet. _____

_____

H. Answer the following questions.

Have you opened up an account with a bank? Which bank? What kind of account have you opened? Have you had a good rate of interest on your savings account? Have you received any interest on your chequing account? What other services offered by the bank have you used? Have you bought a house? Has the bank given you a mortgage? Have you used the bank to obtain a loan? What for? Have you been satisfied with the services offered by the bank? How does banking in Canada compare with banking in your own country?

_____
_____
_____
_____
_____
_____
_____
_____
_____
_____
_____
_____
_____

I. Write a paragraph about some of the things you have done at the bank since you came to Canada. Use present perfect or simple past, as appropriate.

Example: *Since I came to Canada, I have had a lot of reasons to go to the bank . . .*
(open a savings or chequing account; bought a car and needed a loan; applied for a credit card; paid my utility bills, etc.)

_____
_____
_____
_____
_____
_____
_____
_____
_____
_____

Unit III

Present Perfect Progressive

A. Write the progressive form of the present perfect tense.

1. We _____ (go) to the Pancake House for breakfast every Sunday.

2. He can't eat his meal because he _____ (eat) all day long.

3. They _____ (plan) this dinner party for a long time.

4. I _____(diet) for a week now but I haven't lost any weight yet.

5. She _____ (take) cream in her coffee for years.

6. They _____ (see about) the reservation at the restaurant for tonight.

7. You _____ (go) to the Dairy Queen to buy ice cream since you came to Canada.

8. They _____ (go) to McDonalds whenever they have needed to eat a fast meal.

9. I _____ (work) on her birthday cake since Monday.

10. Eating the right food _____ (keep) the children well and happy.

11. Since they came to Canada they _____ (eat) three meals a day.

12. Some of the food that you _____ (look for) from your own country is not available in Canada.

13. The Canada Food Guide _____ (recommend) that we take care to eat a balanced diet.

14. We _____just _____ (eat) dinner.

15. Most grocery stores _____ (open) from 9:30 - 5:30 p.m., but some _____ (stay) open from 7:00 - 11:00 p.m.

16. He likes Chinese food because he _____ (eat) it all his life.

B. Change the verbs to the present perfect progressive if possible. (Remember this is not possible with those verbs that do not have a progressive form.)

1. I haven't eaten any fish this week. _____

_____

2. She has just had her coffee. _____

_____

3. He has not felt well lately, so he has seen a doctor. _____

_____

4. I have known him for many years. _____

5. We have waited for the menu for some time._____

_____

6. They have ordered their soup already. _____

_____

7. Did you enjoy the dessert? _____

8. Has he ever been to the supermarket before? _____

_____

9. I have waited for an hour to begin my lunch._____

_____

10. My friend has gone to Victoria for his vacation this year._____

_____

11. I have looked for a long time for a store that sells saffron._____

_____

12. I have just waved my hand to try and attract the waiter's attention. _____

_____

13. They have already ordered a sandwich. _____

_____

14. He wanted to go to a drive-in restaurant. He had heard a lot about them. _____

_____

15. We are planning to have a picnic. I am seeing to the arrangements for it._____

_____

C. **For each of the sentences below, where possible, write a second sentence using the present perfect progressive of the verb used in the first sentence. Indicate the length of time where necessary.**

Example: I am eating now and I've nearly finished.
I have been eating for half an hour and I've nearly finished.

1. We store food in the freezer section of the refrigerator. It keeps better there. _____

_____

2. Whenever we go to a Chinese restaurant, we try to use chopsticks. _____

_____

3. They have usually bought their flowers at the supermarket. _____

_____

4. I've waited for a long time for the store to open. It hasn't opened yet._____

_____

5. Food stores have for years used refrigeration in Canada._____

_____

6. I went to the supermarket every week. _____

_____

7. There is a store in town which has specialized in selling seafood. _____

_____

8. The small convenience stores open for longer hours than the supermarkets. _____

_____

9. The baker baked the bread all last night._____

_____

10. Because I have tipped the waitress well every time, she gives me good service. _____

_____

D. **Change the following sentences to the present perfect or the present perfect progressive. Substitute the time expression at the left for those which are underlined.**

    Example: *for two weeks*   *He had no need for a refrigerator two weeks ago.*
                      He has had no need for a refrigerator for two weeks.

1. for the last few days   I didn't go shopping <u>last week</u>.

_____

2. Since you came to Canada   <u>When you left your country</u> you changed your eating habits.

_____

_____

3. For a long time   She has eaten dinner <u>already</u>.

_____

4. All year long   They shopped at the small grocery store <u>every day</u>.

_____

_____

5. Since I came   <u>When I came</u> to Canada I learned a lot about the food here.

_____

_____

6. for six weeks   I started to take vitamin pills <u>six weeks ago</u>.

_____

_____

7. before   I never ate cheese <u>in my whole life</u>.

_____

E. **Complete the following sentences with your own ideas using the present perfect progressive tense.**

1. _____ for a week.

2. _____ since Tuesday.

3. _____ all day.

4. _____ for a long time.

5. _____ for almost an hour.

6. _____ all month.

7. _____ since 19___.

8. _____ for twelve years.

9. _____ all my life.

F. Answer the questions in the present perfect progressive where possible.

How long have you waited in this restaurant for your waiter to notice you? Has he been very busy, or has he been talking to a friend and ignoring you? Have you looked at those people at the next table? Have they also waited a long time for service, or has their waiter taken their order and brought them their food?

Have you looked the menu over carefully? And have you decided what you want to order?

How have you enjoyed Canadian food since you came here? Has it been very different from you own food in your country?

_____
_____
_____
_____
_____
_____
_____
_____
_____
_____
_____
_____
_____
_____

G. Write a paragraph on the following subjects, using the present perfect progressive where possible.

1. Ever since I came to Canada, I have been living in . . .

2. Recently, I have been eating three meals a day, each one usually consisting of different kinds of food. For breakfast I have been eating . . .

3. Once a month, as soon as I receive my paycheque, I have been going to the supermarket to buy my groceries. I have been buying . . .

_____
_____
_____
_____
_____
_____
_____
_____

Unit IV

Conditional I

A. Supply the correct tense of the verb making future-possible conditions.

Example: If tomorrow is Sunday, the drug store will not be open.

1. If you _____ (need, go) to the drug store, you _____ (have) to learn the necessary vocabulary.

2. You _____ (take) aspirin if you _____ (have) a headache.

3. If my hair _____ (be) dirty, I _____ (buy) some shampoo.

4. If the pharmacy _____ (be) open at 9:00, I _____ (buy) some medicine.

5. If the pharmacist _____ (not understand) me, he _____ (call) the doctor.

6. I _____ (wear) my sunglasses if the sun _____ (shine).

7. He _____ (look for) some razor blades if he _____ (want) to shave today.

8. If I _____ (want) to find a good magazine or newspaper, I _____ (go) to the drugstore for it.

9. If you _____ (have) a baby, you _____ (find) the drug store useful for your needs.

10. If the drugstore _____ (have) a post-office, she _____ (be able) to buy stamps.

11. If the film _____ (need) developing, the drugstore _____ (do) it.

12. If the doctor _____ (write) special instructions on your prescription, the pharmacist _____ (tell) you.

13. If the clerk _____ (be) new, she _____ (not know) where to find the baby supplies.

14. If you _____ (need) a vaporizer, you _____ (find) it there.

15. If you _____ (ask for) mouthwash, you _____ (have) many kinds to choose from.

16. If they _____ (need) new toothbrushes and toothpaste, they _____ (find) them in the drug store too.

17. If you _____ (cut) your finger, it usually _____ (bleed).

18. I _____ (look for) some candy if I _____ (get to) the drug store before it closes.

19. I _____ (need) some diet aids if I _____ (want) to lose weight.

20. The druggist _____ (sell) you some vitamins if you _____
    (ask for) them.
21. If I _____ (go) to the hospital, I _____ (stay) in a ward.
22. I _____ (need) some crutches if I _____ (break) a leg.
23. You _____ (go) to Emergency if you _____ (need) a doctor
    urgently.
24. If he _____ (have) a lot of headaches, he _____ (see) an eye
    doctor and _____ (have) an eye test.
25. If she _____ (need) prenatal care, she can _____ (get) it at a
    clinic or a hospital.
26. If you _____ (have) heart trouble, you _____ (go) to a
    cardiovascular specialist.

B. Complete the following sentences.
1. The drug store will be open tomorrow if _____.
2. Your teeth will be white if _____.
3. If you want some nail polish, you _____.
4. He won't get a refund if_____.
5. If she needs baby food,_____.
6. I will need some medicine if_____.
7. We will buy soap if _____.
8. Vitamins can help if_____.
9. If he buys some antihistamine_____.
10. If the pharmacist is there, _____.

C. Write sentences containing <u>if</u>-clauses using the words given.
Example: be / on time / dinner / tonight – if / take / cab
I'll be on time for dinner tonight if I take a cab.

1. If/eyes/sore/tomorrow – buy eye-drops

   _____

2. If/go/doctor today – find out/what wrong

   _____

3. If/have/too much wine/dinner tonight – get/sick

   _____

4. If/still/have/earache tomorrow – see/specialist

   _____

5. Must/not/eat/first – if/have/blood test today

   _____

6. If/need/X ray/next week – make/appointment/radiologist

_____

_____

7. Go/pharmacy – if/want/prescription today

_____

8. If/have medical insurance – not/need/pay out/so much money yourself/now

_____

_____

9. If/visit/dentist for check-up/next week – he/X-ray/teeth

_____

D. Combine the following by converting the first sentence into an <u>if</u>-clause.
   Example: *They'll come. We'll see them.*
                If they come, we'll see them.

1. I'll want to clean the bathroom. I will have to buy some cleanser. _____

_____

2. You might break a leg. You will need some crutches. _____

_____

3. She has a really bad allergy. She might need some medicine._____

_____

4. The store is open tomorrow. We will go there._____

_____

5. We should look for laundry supplies. We will be able to do the washing. _____

_____

6. They won't take care. They'll catch cold._____

_____

7. She will want to smell nice. She should buy some perfume. _____

_____

8. It will be your birthday. I will buy you a card and a gift. _____

_____

9. You'll need to buy some medicine. You will have to go to a drug store._____

_____

10. You'll want to buy today's newspaper. You can buy one at the corner. _____

_____

11. He has a cavity. The dentist will fill it. _____

_____

12. The baby needs a vaccination. The mother will take her to the clinic. _____

_____

13. Your brother has a sore throat. Get him some cough drops. _____

_____

E. Answer the following questions using a conditional sentence.

Example: Are you going to buy some make-up?
Yes, if I have enough money, I'll buy some.

1. Do you know a good remedy for a cold? _____

_____

2. Will you come to the doctor with me? _____

_____

3. Who should I see at the hospital? I have broken my arm. _____

_____

4. Will a blood test hurt me? I'm afraid. _____

_____

5. What will you do if your daughter gets sick? _____

_____

6. Will he need something to drink? _____

_____

7. Are you going to have a shot? _____

_____

8. Will you have to go to the dentist? _____

_____

9. Will she need the nurse's help? _____

_____

10. Will I have to go to the clinic for physiotherapy? _____

_____

11. Will the nurse take your blood pressure? _____

_____

12. Will the doctor see her child? _____

_____

13. Will you have a check-up?_____

_____

F. Write two conditional sentences for each of the following.

Example: feel ill
If I feel ill, I go to the doctor.
If I feel ill tomorrow, I'll get some medicine.

1. get wet_____

_____

2. catch a cold_____

_____

3. the doctor is in his office _____

_____

4. the food is bad _____

_____

5. open the window _____

_____

6. stay in bed_____

_____

7. the weather is hot _____

_____

8. be thirsty_____

_____

9. need an ambulance_____

_____

10. want a new pair of shoes_____

_____

11. have a headache _____

_____

12. buy some shampoo _____

_____

13. need some groceries _____

_____

14. go to the bakery_____

_____

G. Answer the questions using a conditional sentence.

Example: *What do you do if you are hungry?*
If I'm hungry, I eat some food.

1. What do you say if someone steps on your foot? _____

_____

2. What do you do if you don't feel well? _____

_____

3. Who do you call if you have an accident and break a leg?_____

_____

4. If you need a prescription, where will you go? _____

_____

5. What do you do if you are thirsty? _____

_____

6. If you are late for an appointment, what do you do? _____

_____

7. Where do you go if you have a toothache?_____

_____

8. What will you do if the drugstore is closed? _____
_____

9. If you are hungry, what do you do? _____
_____

10. If you are getting too fat, what do you do? _____
_____

H. Composition topics.

(a) Suppose you go to the drug store. Mention some of the items you can buy there. Use conditional sentences whenever possible.

Example: If I have a prescription, I'll go to the pharmacy counter.

Suggested Vocabulary:

medicine	exchange	hose/nylons	film
drugs/druggist	vaporizer	baby food	cigarettes
band aids	cosmetics	diapers	candy, chocolate bar
aspirin	lipstick	formula	chewing gum
vitamins	perfume	newspaper	toothbrush/toothpaste
shampoo	nail polish	magazine	mouthwash
refund	hair brush/comb	stationery	

_____
_____
_____
_____
_____
_____
_____
_____
_____
_____
_____
_____
_____
_____
_____
_____
_____
_____
_____
_____
_____
_____
_____

(b) Suppose you are not feeling well. What would you do? How and why? (Use conditional sentences wherever possible).

_____

_____

_____

_____

_____

_____

_____

_____

_____

_____

_____

_____

_____

_____

_____

_____

_____

(c) If you have a toothache, what will you do about it? (Use conditional sentences wherever possible).

_____

_____

_____

_____

_____

_____

_____

_____

_____

_____

_____

_____

_____

_____

_____

_____

_____

_____

Unit V

Time Clauses

A. Fill in the correct time word.

    Example: _____ *I drink coffee, I always take cream and sugar.*
    Whenever I drink coffee, I always take cream and sugar.

1. _____ I feel lonely, I invite friends over for the evening.

2. _____ we finish eating, let's wash the dishes!

3. _____ you first come to Canada, it's hard to make friends if you don't speak the language.

4. I'll put the kettle on for tea _____ he arrives.

5. You make the list of names _____ I write the invitations.

6. _____ you go to someone's home, it is polite to take off your shoes.

7. _____ you have taken off your shoes, you should then take off your coat.

8. I didn't know any Canadians _____ I came to Canada.

9. You can set the table _____ I get the dinner.

10. _____ I return from vacation, I want you and your family to come for Sunday brunch.

11. She forgot to put in any salt _____ she was cooking the potatoes.

12. Tell the children to wash their hands _____ they come to the table.

13. _____ we have dinner at our friends' house, we always take a bottle of wine.

14. _____ the weather improves, let's go on a picnic together!

15. _____ we have eaten, we will go for a walk.

16. One evening, _____ you are free, why don't we go to a movie?

17. _____ I come to your house for dinner, perhaps we should decide whether to make it formal, or just to eat casually.

18. _____ I was eating an oyster, I found a pearl.

19. _____ Lam entered the room, everyone stopped talking.

20. _____ I finish cooking this, we'll sit down and talk.

21. We won't start eating _____ they arrive.

22. Let's have a drink _____ we are waiting.

23. _____ you were out, your friend called.

24. _____ you sit down again, please help me with the dishes.

25. _____ you are in town, you might as well come over for dinner.

26. _____ you are in town, you always come over for dinner.

27. Let's go and visit Maria _____ we have had lunch.

28. _____ I began eating, the telephone rang.

29. She has invited me to dinner often _____ she learned to cook so well.

30. _____ he finished doing the dishes, he left the kitchen.

31. _____ they invite me, it is always a formal occasion.

32. You can bring a friend _____ you come over to the house for tea.

33. Let's stay outside _____ the sun goes down.

34. _____ they invite me, I always make certain I arrive on time.

35. It began to rain _____ we began our picnic.

36. I was so tired, I fell asleep _____ everyone else had a party.

37. _____ the telephone rang, I picked it up.

38. I am happy _____ you are with me!

39. Wash your hands _____ you start cooking.

40. I'll come and visit you _____ I'm in town.

B. Complete the following sentences using time clauses. Use correct punctuation.

Example: *I packed a lunch <u>when we went out for a picnic.</u>*

1. They always come on time _____

2. The soup boiled over _____

3. Come and visit me _____

4. Let's take a vacation together _____

5. I want to introduce you to someone _____

6. Will you call me _____

7. I started learning English _____

8. I used to love Chinese food _____

9. Take off your hat _____

10. I enjoyed getting together _____

11. I'll have some coffee _____

12. Don't go out _____

13. Don't be late _____

C. Fill in the blanks with the appropriate verbs and time words.

_____ I _____ (get) home from work and _____ I _____ (visit) my friend tonight, I _____ (have) a shower and _____ (change) my clothes.

We _____ (plan) to have dinner together at his place and _____ he _____ (cook) it, I _____ (help) by setting the table. He _____ (buy) the food _____ he _____ (get) home from work. _____ I _____ (go) to his place to eat, I always _____ (take) some wine or beer for us to drink.

_____ I _____ (meet) him, I _____ (not have) any friends in Canada.

D. Make sentences using the following words in the main clause and time clause.

Example: (M.C.) come Canada   (T.C.) be ten years old.
I came to Canada when I was ten years old.

Time Clause	Main Clause
1. invite friend for dinner	feel happy
2. eat lunch	have drink
3. arrive home	take shower
4. finish eating	go theatre
5. go park	play tennis
6. move in apartment	neighbor invite coffee
7. arrive here	become friends
8. door locked	not enter house
9. drink tea	boil water
10. have soup	eat salad

E. Answer the following questions using time clauses.

1. When did you come to Canada? _____

_____

2. What subjects have you been studying since you came to Canada? _____

_____

3. Where did you live in your own country? _____

_____

4. What did you do before you came here? _____

_____

5. What happened when you arrived? _____

_____

F. Complete the following sentences using main clauses. Use correct punctuation.

Example: *When we went out for a picnic, I packed a lunch.*

1. Since they invited me_____

2. After I arrived _____

3. When I was nine _____

4. As I was standing there_____

5. Until I met you _____

6. While I was sleeping _____

7. Before I went to visit her_____

8. As soon as I knew _____

9. Before I leave you _____

10. Whenever he visits me_____

11. When you came for coffee _____

12. Immediately before we arrived _____

13. Just before the doorbell rang _____

G. Make one of the sentences into a time clause using the word given to introduce the clause. Note that only in some cases can either sentence be used.

Example: *He was at my house. He ate dinner with us. (when)*
When he was at my house, he ate dinner with us.
He was at my house when he ate dinner with us.

1. Jung speaks English. He visits his Canadian friends. (whenever)_____

_____

2. I go to the theatre. I am in town. (when)_____

_____

3. She invited me to eat with her. She learned to cook. (since) _____

_____

4. Come inside. Take off your shoes. (before) _____

_____

5. We'll have a picnic. It stops raining. (as soon as) _____

_____

6. I go back to my country. I'll see my family. (when)_____

_____

7. The phone rang. We were talking. (while) _____

_____

8. Andrea ate the salad. She ate the soup. (after) _____

_____

9. They are going to stay in Ottawa. His father arrives on Monday. (until) _____

_____

H. Underline the words introducing time clauses in the following paragraph.

When Siwan went to kindergarten, she was only five years old. As soon as she was six, she began first grade and she stayed in primary school until she was eleven. After she reached eleven, she went to Junior High School and she stayed there until she was fifteen. While she was in these schools, she made many friends and whenever they got together at a friend's house, they tried to persuade their parents to allow them to stay the night and sleep there. As long as they went to sleep early, their parents gave them permission because whenever they stayed up too late, the girls always wanted to stay in bed too long the next day. Now Siwan is in High School. As soon as she finishes there, she will go to university. As long as she studies hard and has her good friends, she will be a happy and successful girl.

Write five more sentences about what she will do in university and later in her life, using time clauses wherever possible.

_____
_____
_____
_____
_____
_____
_____
_____
_____
_____

I. Composition: Write a paragraph on each of the following using time clauses where possible.

1. What happened on the day you came to Canada?

2. What do you do when you get together with a friend for the evening?

3. What do you do when you leave the class?

_____
_____
_____
_____
_____
_____
_____
_____
_____
_____
_____

_____
_____
_____
_____
_____
_____
_____
_____
_____
_____
_____
_____
_____
_____
_____
_____
_____
_____
_____

J. Write a paragraph describing how you entertain friends in your country, using as many time clauses as possible.

Example: _When my friends arrive, they take off their shoes._

_____
_____
_____
_____
_____
_____
_____
_____
_____
_____
_____
_____
_____

Unit VI

Relative Clauses

A. Substitute the words in the left column for those words in the sentences that are underlined. Use the correct form of the verb and correct punctuation.

Example: cars / sell   *This is the <u>house</u> I wanted to <u>buy</u>.*
                                    These are the cars I wanted to sell.

1. girls/daughters   The <u>child</u> that is so pretty is my <u>grandchild</u>.

_____

2. Mosque/day   This is the <u>church</u> that I attend every <u>Sunday</u>.

_____

3. weakest/fight   The <u>strongest</u> man that I have ever <u>seen</u> is your father.

_____

4. uncle/arrival   These are the <u>friends</u> whose <u>tickets</u> we were waiting for.

_____

5. schools/far away   The <u>shop</u> which we go to is <u>near here</u>.

_____

6. Mr. Anderson/cousin   <u>The man</u> whose house is next to yours is a <u>friend of mine.</u>

_____

B. Combine the following sentences. Change the second one into a relative clause using the appropriate pronoun. Add the clause either at the end of the sentence or in the place indicated with *.

Example: *Our teacher wrote a textbook. *We are using it.*
               Our teacher wrote a textbook which we are using.

1. You must telephone the parents. Their children are not in school. _____

_____

2. Those two girls * are twins. You see them._____

_____

3. My father * is an old man. He lives with my brother and his wife. _____

_____

4. His sister has worked for the airline. It flies from Vancouver to Toronto. _____

_____

5. This apartment * is mine. You can see it._____

_____

6. This is the playground. The children can play in it. _____

_____

7. All my family * are going. They are living in Canada. _____

_____

8. That is her aunt. She was telling us about her. _____

_____

9. My sister * has a lot of work to do. She has two jobs. _____

_____

10. I talked to the woman. Her son is my teacher. _____

_____

11. He is buying a condominium. It has four bedrooms. _____

_____

12. All his family are working in their own restaurant. It is in Edmonton. _____

_____

13. I spoke to the man. He is the French professor. _____

_____

14. She's wearing the blue dress. She added some silver buttons to it. _____

_____

15. The skirt * is too short. I borrowed it. _____

_____

16. Many people * are Christian. They live in Canada. _____

_____

17. His winter jacket * is not warm enough for below-zero weather. It is made of nylon. _____

_____

_____

18. We received a letter from our mother. She lives a long way away. _____

_____

19. I like her shorts. They are exactly right for summer. _____

_____

20. My sister * is only twenty. She is divorced. _____

_____

21. That lady * is my grandmother. I was talking to her in the hall. _____

_____

22. My bathing suit * is too small. I bought it last year. _____

_____

23. You are the nicest person. I know you. _____

_____

24. The house * is old. I am living in it. _____

_____

25. I will be wearing a black dress. It has white buttons and a white collar. _____

_____

26. A priest * married them. He had known them for a long time. _____

_____

C. Complete the following partial statements. Write a full sentence using the words given with a relative clause.

Example: *first day that*
           I'll never forget the first day (that) I came to Canada.

1. a mother whose _____

_____

2. a friend who _____

_____

3. families that _____

_____

4. the city (in) which _____

_____

5. a brother whose _____

_____

6. a dog that _____

_____

7. the son (for) whom _____

_____

8. all the people who _____

_____

9. the minister (to) whom _____

_____

10. the church (to) which _____

_____

11. an apartment that _____

_____

12. the street where _____

_____

13. the best person that _____

_____

14. a daughter-in-law (with) whom _____

_____

15. the year when _____

_____

16. the student whom _____ _____

17. the country where _____

18. the reason why_____

D. Read the following paragraphs and then answer the questions using relative clauses.

Example: My sister goes to the office. She works there.
What office?   The office where my sister works.

(a) My brother often takes the 8:00 bus to work. This is a fast non-stop bus. If he misses this bus, he has to take a slower one at 8:15. John is his friend. He goes to work with my brother. If my brother is not on the bus, John sits beside another friend, Peter. He goes to work on the bus too.

1. What is the 8:00?_____

2. What kind of bus is it? _____

3. What is the 8:15?_____

4. Who is John? _____

5. Who is Peter? _____

(b) In Canada, the nuclear (or immediate) family usually consists of a mother and father and one or two children. Canadian parents love their children and the child-raising is taken care of by the parents without the help of the extended family members such as aunts, uncles, cousins and grandparents.

Frequently, mothers go to work and put young children in daycare, which provides a good, healthy environment. Children often have a room of their own, to give them privacy when they need it. Once they have passed the stages of adolescence and puberty, they are free to choose their own lifestyle and career, although the parents try to help them as much as they can.

The nuclear family generally stays together until the children reach the ages of 18-21, when they are encouraged to move out and begin an independent life of their own.

Members of the older generation seldom live with the immediate family but prefer, instead, to maintain their own independence by living in a retirement home or community where they can mix with their own age group and enjoy life with their peers.

1. What is the nuclear or immediate family unit in Canada?_____

2. Who raises the children?_____

3. What is the extended family?_____

4. What does daycare provide and when is it used? _____

5. Why are children sometimes given a room of their own? _____

6. What happens after adolescence and puberty? _____

_____

7. At what age does the nuclear family break up?_____

_____

8. Where do the members of the older generation usually live?_____

_____

E. Write about the nuclear and extended family customs in your country.

_____
_____
_____
_____
_____
_____
_____
_____
_____
_____
_____
_____
_____
_____
_____
_____

F. Composition: Bring a photograph of your family or friends, or draw a picture if you don't have a photograph available. Describe the people in the picture, using relative clauses.

Example: *The man who is standing at the back of the photo is my father. My mother, who is wearing a blue sweater, is a very gentle person.*

_____
_____
_____
_____
_____
_____
_____
_____
_____
_____
_____
_____
_____

G. Below is a sample composition. Read it, and then write a similar composition about your own family.

I want to tell you about the members of my family who are living in Canada. My mother and father, who came here in 1978, are living on a farm which is situated in Alberta. My older brother, who is also living and working on the farm, came to Canada two years after they did. His wife, who is Canadian, is living there too.

My older sister, who is divorced, is living with her two children on Vancouver Island. She works at Butchart Gardens, which is a very beautiful place. The children, who go to school during the day, often help her in the evenings.

My younger sister is here in Toronto with me. She and I are both working in jobs which we like very much. At night, which is the only time we have free, we both take English classes.

Unit VII

Modals (Present/Future), Polite Requests

A. Fill in the blanks with appropriate modals.

1. _____ I use the copy machine, please?
2. The librarian _____ be able to help you, I'm sure.
3. You _____ get check-out slips at the counter.
4. If he needs to get a book, he _____ go to the public library.
5. _____ you help her? She wants to know how she _____ find it.
6. Yes. First she _____ look it up in the library catalogue and she _____ write down the call number.
7. Then she _____ go to the shelves and she _____ probably find it without difficulty.
8. Once she has found the book, she _____ take it to the check-out counter.
9. The librarian _____ check it out for her.
10. Books _____ always be returned on or before the date they are due.
11. I_____ find a book about whales.
12. Where _____ I go look for it?
13. How long _____ you generally keep a book out?
14. _____ we check out any book we want?
15. What other services _____ the library offer besides checking out books?
16. Perhaps you _____ find periodicals there and copy machines. Some libraries also _____ have audio tapes, CDs and videos available.
17. In any case, everything in a library that _____ be checked out _____ have a call number for reference.
18. Many libraries have a place where you _____ sit down and read.
19. He _____ get this book today because he _____ study tonight.
20. People _____ not talk in a loud voice in a library. It is a place where they _____ be quiet.

B. Complete the following.

1. I should go to the library because _____
2. I ought to reserve the book because _____
3. I had better call the librarian because_____
4. I should go to the library catalogue because _____
5. I must use the photocopier because _____
6. I might borrow a CD because_____

C. Give advice by using <u>had better</u>, <u>ought to</u> and <u>should</u>.

Example: I can't find the book I need.   You should ask the librarian.

1. He can't see where the newspapers are. _____

_____

2. There is too much noise and he isn't able to study. _____

_____

3. She doesn't know how to use the photocopier. _____

_____

4. I can't get the encyclopedia down from the shelf. _____

_____

5. I can't find the card catalogue. _____

_____

6. He doesn't know where the CDs are kept. _____

_____

7. They can't see the reference desk. _____

_____

8. I don't know where the non-fiction section is. _____

_____

9. The child wants the children's books but he can't find them. _____

_____

D. Write in the negative.

1. He can read the book. _____

2. Can you talk in a library? _____

3. Could he find the card? _____

4. She may find the correct reference. _____

_____

5. You might like that novel. _____

6. If you want to find someone's life story, you should look for it in the biographical section.

_____

_____

7. It's Sunday. The library ought to be open today. _____

_____

8. You must make a lot of noise here. _____

_____

9. He has to find the correct card. _____

E. Look at the following sentences and say whether <u>must</u> means (a) necessity, (b) warning, (c) assumption.

1. They must read those books by next week. _____

2. I recognize that person. I must know her. _____

3. You must be there before he leaves. _____

4. They are putting the lights out. It must be time to close. _____

5. You must be quiet! (If you aren't, you'll have to leave.) _____

F. Look at the following sentences and say whether <u>could</u> means (a) permission, (b) possibility, (c) request, (d) doubt.

1. Could I get a library book out today? _____

2. You could go now but it probably won't be open. _____

3. Could you help me with this call number? _____

4. You could use the library once you have a card. _____

5. You could borrow my dictionary if you like. _____

6. Could you come with me? _____

G. Look at the following sentences and say whether <u>will</u> means (a) future tense, (b) request, (c) promise.

1. I will read the newspaper while you look for a book. _____

2. Will you show me where the card catalogue is? _____

3. Tomorrow is a holiday. The library will be closed. _____

4. I will definitely be there to meet you. _____

5. Will you return this book for me please? _____

H. Look at the following sentences and say whether <u>should</u> means (a) advisability, (b) expectation, (c) assumption.

1. We should check to see if it is open before going. _____

2. I've found the call number. It should be on the shelf. _____

3. Should we ask for a call slip? _____

4. It's 10:00 a.m. The library should be open. _____

5. It's nice and quiet here. It should be a good place to study. _____

I. Look at the following sentences and say whether <u>would</u> means (a) request, (b) preference, (c) desire, (d) future uncertainty.

1. Would you please reserve this book for me? _____

2. I would enjoy reading a magazine from my own country. _____

3. Would you like to have this novel in paperback? _____

4. I would rather find it in hard cover. _____

5. I would study harder if I thought it would help! _____

J. Write a paragraph on how to make use of the library. Use as many modals as possible.
You can begin: If you want to join your local library, you <u>must</u> obtain a library card first.

_____
_____
_____
_____
_____
_____
_____
_____
_____
_____
_____
_____
_____
_____
_____
_____
_____
_____
_____
_____
_____
_____

K. Use a modal to express the following ideas.

1. Go to the library (ability) _____
_____

2. Check out some CDs from the library (possibility) _____
_____

3. Bring the books back on time (advisability) _____
_____

4. Finish this book today (expectation) _____
_____

5. A good book (assumption) _____

6. Go to the periodical section before leaving (necessity) _____
_____

7. I like non-fiction better than fiction (preference) _____
_____

8. Cover the books up, it's raining (advisability) _____
_____

9. The library is open until 9:00 p.m. tomorrow (future) _____

_____

10. I don't buy the newspaper. I read it in the library (preference) _____

_____

11. I want to check out this book (desire) _____

_____

12. The book has been returned late. Pay a fine (necessity) _____

_____

13. Take the children to the library (possibility) _____

_____

14. Borrow a book (ability) _____

15. See a film at the local library (possibility) _____

_____

L. Fill in the blanks with an appropriate modal.

Example: You (should) read that book. (advisability)

1. We _____ go there tomorrow. (possibility)

2. You _____ like that story. (possibility)

3. It _____ be open. (expectation)

4. They ordered the book for me, so it _____ be there today. (assumption)

5. We _____ try to find the newspaper but it's very old and I doubt if it is here. (doubt)

6. The bus _____ stop in front of the building. (expectation)

7. If you don't want to pay a fine you _____ return the book right away. (advisability)

8. I _____ read science fiction. (preference)

9. _____ I help you? (asking assent)

10. He _____ read the newspaper every day. (advisability)

11. I _____ like to have a library card, please. (desire)

12. I can't find the book in the library so I _____ buy it. (necessity)

13. The book _____ be here next week. (future)

14. It is closed. It _____ be open at 10:00, however. (expectation)

15. I think I have read all the books by that author but he _____ write another one soon. (possibility)

16. _____ she read well? (ability)

17. _____ she borrow that book? (permission)

18. We _____ return the book by Friday. (necessity)

19. It _____ be open tomorrow. (possibility)

20. Everyone _____ obey the rules and sit quietly. (necessity)

M. Add the word <u>to</u> where appropriate, otherwise put an <u>X</u>.

1. You must _____ read this book.

2. I have _____ talk to the librarian.

3. I would rather _____ use this dictionary.

4. He ought _____ study harder.

5. They should _____ finish the story.

6. You can _____ pay the fine here.

7. We may _____ borrow books often.

8. You have _____ return them within two weeks.

9. I had better _____ read this book first.

10. We have _____ find two books about Canada.

11. I will _____ buy this paperback.

12. There are several librarians here who can _____ help you.

13. We might _____ want this one again next week.

14. You have got _____ do it.

15. We will _____ go to the library first.

16. I would _____ like to read this.

17. I can _____ borrow records with my library card.

18. Children should _____ learn to enjoy reading.

19. You have got _____ read that book! It's wonderful.

20. We have _____ study at the library tonight.

N. Ask polite questions for the situations given below.

Example: *You want to make a photocopy and need some change.*
Could you change a dollar bill, please?

1. You ask the librarian if you can join the library. _____

_____

2. You want to use a dictionary that someone else is using. _____

_____

3. You want to meet your teacher at the bus stop in front of the library at 2:00. _____

_____

4. You want to ask the librarian to help you use the computer. _____

_____

5. You call the library on the telephone. You want to know when it is open. _____

_____

6. You want to know if you can use the photocopier. Ask the librarian. _____

_____

7. You want to know if you can take a reference book home. _____

_____

8. You want to use a table for studying in the library._____

_____

9. You want the librarian to order you a book from another library. _____

_____

10. You are the librarian. You offer a book to someone that you think she would like to read.

_____

O. Write a paragraph about some things you <u>could</u> do, <u>should</u> do, <u>might</u> do or <u>ought to</u> do in a library.

_____
_____
_____
_____
_____
_____
_____
_____
_____
_____
_____
_____
_____
_____
_____
_____
_____
_____
_____
_____
_____
_____
_____
_____
_____
_____
_____
_____
_____
_____
_____
_____
_____
_____
_____
_____
_____

Unit VIII

Coordination – Compound Sentences

A. Combine the following into one sentence using coordinating conjunctions.
   Example: *I wrote the letter. I mailed the letter.*
   I wrote and mailed the letter.

1. Write the letter. Put the letter in an envelope. _____

_____

2. Seal the envelope. Put a stamp on it. _____

_____

3. Put the stamp on the right-hand corner of the envelope. Address the envelope. _____

_____

_____

4. We are sending a postcard. We don't need an envelope. _____

_____

5. I sent an air letter. I didn't need an envelope. _____

_____

6. He didn't have an airmail envelope. He wrote "air mail" on the envelope. _____

_____

_____

7. We didn't receive a letter from home. We didn't receive a postcard. (Note that when you use <u>nor,</u> the sentence following it must be in the affirmative to avoid the use of double negatives.) _____

_____

_____

8. They wanted to pick up some registered mail. They didn't have any identification on them. They had to go home to get it. _____

_____

_____

9. I requested my mail be redirected. I am moving to a new address. _____

_____

10. Most residential areas have their branch office of the Post Office. Just choose the one nearest to you. _____

_____

_____

11. I like receiving letters. I don't like writing letters. _____

_____

12. Please write bigger. Please write more clearly. _____

_____

B. Insert the correct form of the verb <u>to be</u> in the blanks.

1. Not only a letter, but also a parcel _____ waiting for you.

2. Either the mailman or the Post Office van _____ going to deliver the package.

3. Both the stamp and the address _____ important when mailing a letter.

4. Not only the domestic mail, but also foreign mail _____ expensive.

5. Neither air mail stickers nor special delivery stickers _____ going to cost you any money.

6. Whether the package goes air mail or surface _____ unimportant.

7. Not only the address, but also the postal code _____ important.

8. Both letter and parcel rates _____ going up.

C. Rewrite the following using a variety of paired conjunctions.

Example: *You have written the letter. You haved mailed it.*
   I've both written the letter and mailed it.
   I've neither written nor mailed the letter.

1. You must write an air letter. You must send a telegram. _____

_____

2. He doesn't write letters. He doesn't receive letters. _____

_____

3. You are going to the Post Office. You are also going to the library. _____

_____

4. You have met our postman. You have met his dog. _____

_____

5. He has your letter. She has your letter. _____

_____

6. I don't receive letters. I don't write letters. _____

_____

7. The letter was mailed. The parcel was mailed. _____

_____

8. The letter needs a stamp. It also needs an address. _____

_____

9. It makes no difference if you walk or ride to the Post Office. It's close by. _____

_____

10. You haven't written to anyone lately. I haven't written to anyone lately. _____

_____

11. She didn't buy any envelopes. She didn't buy any stamps. _____

_____

12. You go and talk to the Postmaster. I will go and talk to the Postmaster. _____

_____

13. I wrapped the parcel. I mailed the parcel. _____

_____

14. He bought the new edition of stamps and also the Christmas stamps. _____

_____

D. Fill the the blanks with a correct verb or modal form.
   Example: He writes a lot of letters, and so <u>do</u> I.

1. Post Offices exist everywhere in Canada, and so _____ couriers.
2. Letters may be sent anywhere in the world, and _____ parcels.
3. They have finished writing their postcards, and so _____ we.
4. You drugstore has a Post Office in it, and so _____ ours.
5. He had to go to the Post Office, and so _____ I.
6. You didn't mail any Christmas cards this year, and neither _____ I.
7. I sent a postcard from Ottawa and he _____ too.
8. It doesn't matter whether you write in the address or I _____ .
9. He will write a letter and so _____ she.
10. I haven't written home this week and neither _____ you.

E. Finish the incomplete sentences with clauses introduced by <u>so</u>, <u>and</u>, <u>or</u>, <u>but</u>, <u>for</u>, <u>yet</u>, <u>nor</u>. Punctuate correctly.
   Example: He writes lots of letters.
   He writes lots of letters, yet he never receives any.

1. I was waiting for a parcel _____
2. He was in a hurry _____
3. You can either telephone_____
4. We needed some stamps _____
5. I haven't heard from my parents_____
6. She collects stamps_____
7. He can neither read _____
8. She hates to write letters _____
9. The package is at the Post Office _____
10. Change of address forms used to be free _____
11. We need some airletters _____
12. I sent some Christmas cards _____

F. Does (a) or (b) coordinate better?

1. He had written a letter,

_____(a) but the package was lost.
_____(b) but he forgot to mail it.

2. She was busily looking for the Customs Declaration,

_____(a) for she needed it before she could send the parcel abroad.
_____(b) for it needed both an envelope and a stamp.

3. The letter never got there because I put neither

_____(a) a money order in it nor a piece of paper.
_____(b) a stamp on it nor an address on the envelope.

4. I addressed the airletter clearly,

_____(a) yet it never reached its destination.
_____(b) yet it arrived without difficulty.

5. You must get the right change,

_____(a) or the letters won't be sent.
_____(b) or you won't get a stamp from the stamp machine.

6. The stamps were cheap,

_____(a) so they didn't cost much.
_____(b) so I bought plenty of them for future use.

7. I didn't write to him,

_____(a) nor did I telephone.
_____(b) nor did he come and visit me.

G. Agree with the statement. Use <u>so</u> or <u>neither</u>.

Example: I'm going to the Post Office.
So am I.

1. I got a letter. _____

2. I didn't write home. _____

3. I must send a post card. _____

4. I needed a stamp. _____

5. I don't want any air letters. _____

6. I would like a money order. _____

7. I'm walking to the Post Office._____

8. I couldn't help reading her letter. _____

H. Write a short composition about (a) mailing a letter within your own country, (b) comparing post office facilities there with the facilities here in Canada. Use as many compound sentences as possible and all the conjunctions you can.

_____
_____
_____
_____
_____
_____
_____
_____
_____
_____
_____
_____
_____
_____
_____
_____
_____
_____
_____
_____
_____
_____
_____
_____
_____
_____
_____
_____
_____
_____
_____
_____
_____
_____

Unit IX

Modals (past)

A. For each of the following situations, tell what someone shouldn't have done, and then what they should have done.

Example: *Tan came to school without his books.*
He shouldn't have come without his books.
He should have brought his books to school.

1. Billy told the teacher a lie. The teacher got very angry. _____

_____

2. You didn't study for your test; instead, you watched TV all evening. You failed the test.

_____

_____

3. Mary didn't do her homework last night. She went to the movie instead. The teacher gave her "zero". _____

_____

4. The registration date for the course was September 20. I went to register on September 22. The course was full. _____

_____

5. You overslept this morning. You didn't get up on time. You were late for school. _____

_____

_____

6. Katya didn't put her son in kindergarten. She kept him at home. Now she's sorry because he doesn't have any friends to play with. _____

_____

7. I didn't study biology in high school; instead I studied German. Now I'm sorry because I can't enter a nursing course. _____

_____

8. You went to school yesterday instead of staying in bed. You had a high fever and felt very unwell. _____

_____

9. I didn't learn English when I was younger. I was too lazy. Now it's very difficult for me.

_____

_____

10. Nick was rude to the teacher. _____

_____

11. Professor Woods gave the students an important test. He didn't warn them._____

_____

B. Fill in the blanks with the past form of <u>ought to</u> or <u>should.</u>

1. You (study) _____ English before you came here.

2. Maren (eat) _____ breakfast before she went to school.

3. Tim (sit) _____ close to the blackboard because his eyesight was poor.

4. You wanted to pass the course but you didn't study. You (study) _____ harder.

5. Suzanna likes to play sports. She didn't take sports at school. She (take) _____ physical education.

6. I (use) _____ a dictionary to write my composition because I made several spelling mistakes.

7. I'm moving to Montreal. I (take) _____ a French course when I was at school.

8. Bob didn't enrol for the class because he was broke. He (apply) _____ for a scholarship.

9. Henry can't afford the fees this term. He (work) _____ in the summer and on weekends.

10. I (get) _____ a calendar from the college in order to plan my timetable.

C. Use the progressive form of the past modals <u>ought to</u> and <u>should</u> to complete the following.

Example: *You were talking to the other students during class. You (should have been paying) attention to the teacher.*

1. We were watching TV. We had an exam the next day. We (study) _____ for the exam.

2. He (not eat) _____ candy in the classroom while the teacher was showing slides. It was against the rules.

3. Peter (not use) _____ a calculator during his math test.

4. You (not copy) _____ from your friend during the exam. The teacher will give you a "zero" for cheating.

5. She (listen) _____ to the teacher. She was whispering to her friend. Now she doesn't understand the assignment.

6. It was too late to learn all the work for the test yesterday. You (study) _____ all term.

D. Rewrite a sentence for each of the following situations telling you what to assume.

Example: *John took a TOEFL test last August. It's September and he's enrolling at university. He must have done well on his TOEFL test.*

1. Jay usually has a class at 10:00. It's 10:05 and he's still drinking coffee in the cafeteria.

2. Maria went to her first English class yesterday. She wants to transfer to a higher level.

_____

3. The teacher is handing back the exam papers. (a) She is smiling at John as she returns his paper. (b) She is frowning at Betty. _____

_____

_____

4. Sherry was playing tennis at lunchtime. Now she's in the nurse's office and is getting a bandage on her head._____

_____

5. Paul took a provincial test for mechanics last month. He now has a good job at a service station downtown. _____

_____

6. Why was Karen running to class? _____

7. Tashi said she might move to another town. She hasn't been at school for a week._____

_____

8. Don was in grade eight last year. Now he's in grade nine._____

_____

9. Why did Toni's father go to the school to see the principal?_____

_____

10. Why is Fran crying? _____

11. Tran was looking for a job. I haven't seen him for a long time._____

_____

12. Kristin's knee is bleeding. She was on the swings in the playground._____

_____

13. Joanne looked at the book. She began to laugh. _____

_____

E. Use the correct past tense form of <u>have to (must)</u> in the sentences below.

Example: She was six years old, so she (attend) <u>had to attend</u> school

1. He was hurt badly playing hockey, so they (take/him) _____ to the hospital.

2. Because he wanted to work as a plumber, he (write) _____ an inter-provincial exam.

3. She was a mature student so she (not/have) _____ a high school diploma in order to study at the university.

4. Mai (not/pay) _____ in order to attend school last year.

5. (pay/you) _____ in order to attend school in your country?

6. Before you started school (have/you) _____ proof of citizenship?

7. When we lived in Ontario we (pay) _____ property taxes which provided money for education.

8. You (return) _____ from your holiday at the end of August last year in order to start school on time.

9. Who (you/tell) _____ that you would be absent from school?

F. Fill in the blanks with <u>could not have + past participle</u> to express impossibility.

Example: He (study) <u>couldn't have studied</u> medicine because his marks were too low.

1. Tony (cheat) _____ on the exam because he's so honesst.

2. Marta (quit) _____ school because she's only fourteen.

3. You (arrive) _____ on time since you left at 8:55.

4. He said he saw me at the parent-teacher interviews but he (see/me) _____ because I was at work.

5. My daughter (get) _____ a high score on the literature test since she's just started to learn English.

6. You (register) _____ for a daytime class since you work every afternoon.

7. Roberto (go) _____ away to college since his wife is taking courses here.

8. He (work) _____ as a teacher. His documents hadn't been translated evaluated.

G. Tell what <u>could (or couldn't) have happened</u> in the following situations.

Example: Margaret hasn't arrived at school yet. She could have missed the bus.
I haven't seen Margaret this morning. She couldn't have arrived yet.

1. The teacher was in a bad mood. _____

2. You usually do well on your tests. You did poorly on yesterday's test. _____
_____

3. Jean studied in an English school. There are also bilingual schools in this city. _____
_____

4. Louise has a 3 year old daughter who stays home with her every day. There's a nursery school close by. _____
_____

5. Preregistration for the course was last Tuesday. You registered yesterday. _____
_____

6. Fees can be paid in two installments. You paid the entire fee at one time. _____
_____

7. You wanted to attend the class but you didn't have any money. _____
_____

8. You were excellent in drafting at school; however, you dropped the course. _____
_____

9. You didn't try hard in that class so your grades were low._____

_____

10. Since Helga didn't know how to spell a word, she made a mistake in her composition.

_____

H. Fill in the blanks with <u>could (or couldn't) have been + present participle</u>.

Example: I didn't see Mary when I went to her home.
She <u>could have been doing</u> her homework.

1. The teacher took away the student's exam paper. The student _____

_____

2. The students wanted to drop out of the course. They _____
_____trouble with the course.

3. Eve went to the principal's office for her punishment. She _____
_____ in class.

4. Linda spent a lot of time in the library yesterday. She_____

_____

5. Why didn't you study French in high school? You _____
_____ another language while you were studying other subjects.

6. Elizabeth_____ because she is the best student in class.

7. Although you were working during the day, you _____
math at night school.

8. You stayed at school late last night. When I saw you, you were drinking coffee with your
friends. You _____ your homework.

I. Answer the following questions using <u>may (might) (not) have + past participle</u>.

Example: Why did she repeat grade nine?
She might (may) have found it difficult.
She might (may) not have understood the work.

1. Why were many students absent yesterday?_____

_____

2. Why did Peter get a headache before he went to school every day last year? _____

_____

3. Why did the student rewrite the composition? _____

_____

4. Why did the teacher talk to Yumiko?_____

_____

5. Why did he transfer to another class? _____

_____

6. Why did she stop coming to school? _____

_____

7. Why did Binh take her child to a day care? _____

_____

8. Why did Susan make so many mistakes? _____

_____

9. Why did Alain miss four weeks of class? _____

_____

10. Why was Isabelle yawning in class? _____

_____

J. Fill in the blanks with <u>would rather have (+ past participle)</u> or <u>would have liked to (+simple form of the infinitive)</u>.

Example: I <u>would have liked to study</u> (study) geography but I couldn't because the class was full.

1. Mary _____ (go) to school in the daytime instead of the evening but she couldn't because of her job.

2. Juan _____ (take) credit courses but he couldn't until his English improved.

3. I don't like Math but I had to take it. I _____ (study) Chemistry.

4. _____ you _____ (have) Miss Smith than Mr. Anderson for a teacher?

5. You _____ (learn) to sew at night school but the course wasn't offered last term.

6. We _____ (hear) a speaker than watched a movie in class yesterday. The movie was boring.

7. Tom _____ (take) a vocational course but his parents insisted he go to university.

8. _____ you _____ (study) at a bilingual school when you were a student?

K. In the following sentences, give appropriate modals for the meaning given in brackets.

Example: (necessity) He <u>had to pay</u> (pay) his tuition last Monday.

1. (ability) You _____ (do) much better work when you were younger.

2. (possibility) John _____ (go) home because he was complaining about a stomach ache this morning.

3. (preference) I _____ (study) Chemistry than Physics when I was in high school.

4. (assumption) Since Susan had high marks in Physical Education she _____ (enjoy) sports.

5. (advisability) You _____ (register) for the course last week. It's too late now.

6. (desire) I _____ (apply) for a scholarship but there were no applications left.

7. (expectation) John _____ (do) well on his exam because he seemed to know the material. I'm surprised he failed.

8. (necessity) _____ you _____ (bring) your passport when your registered for this course?

9. (ability) Mary _____ (play) the piano very well when she was a child.

10. (impossibility) I wish I could have studied English years ago but I _____ (study) it because there were no English teachers in my town.

11. (advisability) You registered for an advanced carpentry class but you've never studied carpentry before. You _____ (register) for that class.

L. Write a past form modal sentence about a past event for each of the following.

Example: *You must study hard in school because you have good grades.*
You must have studied hard in school because you had good grades.

1. You should take a night school course in sewing. You _____ a sewing class years ago.

2. Nick could not have much homework in grade five because he never brings his books home. He _____ much homework in grade four either because we never saw his books.

3. That class must be interesting. The one before it _____ too.

4. You should know the answer to this question. You _____ the answer to the other question too.

5. You shouldn't interrupt the teacher when she's talking to the class. She gets angry with you. You _____ when she was talking to the class yesterday.

6. We ought to register for the next course. We _____ for the last course because it sounded interesting.

7. The teacher might help you if you ask him. He _____ yesterday, too.

M. Answer the following questions using past form modals.

Example: *I can't find my homework. What could have happened to it?*
You could have left it on the bus on your way to school.

1. Why might Marta have failed the test?_____

2. Luong's friends always bought their lunch at the school cafeteria. He always brought his lunch. What would he have liked to do? _____

_____

3. My sister wanted to be a secretary. What course should she have taken? _____

_____

4. My friend wanted to work but she had a small baby. What could she have done? _____

_____

5. The teacher took a student's test paper away and gave him "zero". What must the student have been doing? _____

_____

6. Katya wanted to apply for university. What did she have to do in order to register?

_____

7. None of the children went to school on Thursday. Why must that have been? _____

_____

8. Tom was very nervous before his exam. What might have been the reason? _____

_____

9. Kiem didn't know what to do because her children were having two weeks' Christmas vacation. She had to work. What could she have done about her children? _____

_____

N. Comment on each of the following situations. Use the past form of the modals given.

Example: *It was difficult going to school full-time (would rather)*
I would rather have gone to school part-time.

1. Sal didn't go to school this morning. (must) _____

_____

2. John skipped school last Friday. The principal caught him. (should) _____

_____

3. Why is the teacher so pleased with Max? (could) _____

_____

4. The principal expelled one of my classmates. (must) _____

_____

5. Why didn't Andrew graduate? (may) _____

_____

6. Why did you do military service? (have to) _____

_____

7. You made a lot of mistakes on your essay. (should) _____

_____

8. I wanted to learn ceramics last year. (could) _____

_____

9. During the English class Maria was speaking Spanish. (ought to) _____

_____

10. The teacher was late this morning. (might) _____

_____

11. The students wanted to transfer to a lower class. (may)_____

_____

12. Thomas was lonely when he went to school. (might not) _____

_____

13. After Betty began school, her English improved a lot. (must) _____

_____

O. Write a paragraph telling about the education you received in your country. Use as many past tense modals as possible. Discuss any of the following topics.
Primary and Secondary School

Post Secondary School

Was education compulsory? For what ages and when? What were the levels of school? What kinds of school could one attend? What kinds of Post Secondary schools were there? Who could attend? Who paid for education? What were the requirements for students? Was there military service?

_____

_____

_____

_____

_____

_____

_____

_____

_____

_____

_____

_____

_____

_____

_____

_____

_____

_____

_____

_____

_____

_____

P. **Using a calendar from a local night school, write about the course you could have taken, the prerequisites, fees, dates, times and content of the courses. What courses were not open to you? Why? State that even though it is too late this term, perhaps you will consider taking a leisure course next term.**

_____

_____

_____

_____

_____

_____

_____

_____

_____

_____

_____

_____

_____

_____

_____

_____

_____

_____

_____

_____

_____

_____

_____

_____

_____

_____

_____

_____

_____

_____

Unit X

Hidden Questions

NW bsmt. apt. Liv. rm. kitch.
bedrm. 4-pc. bath. frig. & stove
On major bus routes
Avail. immed. Ph. 555-3121

A. You are looking for an apartment to rent. You've just seen this advertisement and are telephoning to inquire about the apartment. Complete the following hidden questions, then add your own.

Example: I'd like to know how much the rent is.

1. _____ where _____
2. _____ when _____
3. _____ how many rooms _____
4. _____ what floor _____
5. _____ what appliances _____
6. _____ if (whether) _____ furnished (or not).
7. _____ if _____ damage deposit.
8. _____ if children _____
9. _____ if _____ laundry facilities.
10. _____ if utilities _____
11. _____ if _____ a lease.
12. _____ if pets _____
13. _____
14. _____
15. _____

B. Write these direct questions. Use the expressions given. Be sure to punctuate correctly.

1. What is a security deposit? (I'd like to know)_____

_____

2. How do I get my security deposit back? (Do you know)_____

_____

3. Can the landlord keep my security deposit? (Can you tell me) _____

_____

4. When does the landlord usually collect the rent? (I'm interested in knowing) _____

_____

5. What must a tenant do when he rents an apartment? (Do you happen to know) _____

_____

6. Do I have to pay property tax? (Who knows) _____

_____

7. What are the duties of the landlord? (Please tell me) _____

_____

8. Did the tenant have to obey the landlord's rules? (I wonder)_____

_____

9. How much notice must a landlord give before he raises the rent? (Ask him) _____

_____

10. What is a lease? (Would you mind telling me) _____

_____

11. Do all landlords give leases? (I'm interested in knowing) _____

_____

12. Can a tenant leave before his lease expires? (Do you happen to know)_____

_____

13. When should I tell the landlord that I want to move? (I'm not sure) _____

_____

14. Can he refuse to rent a vacant apartment to me? (Where can I find out)_____

_____

15. How much were the utility bills? (Does anyone know) _____

_____

16. Which utilities did you pay for? (Let me know) _____

_____

17. Where should he go if he has a problem with his landlord? (He'd like to know) _____

_____

18. What condition must I leave the apartment in when I leave? (Ask him) _____

_____

19. Can the landlord enter my apartment if I am not at home? (I can't tell you) _____

_____

20. Are the neighbors noisy? (Who do I tell) _____

_____

C. Complete the following paragraph with indirect questions.

I've learned a few things about renting an apartment. I know how _____
_____ I also know when _____ and of
course I know who _____. I remember what _____

_____?
Do you know who _____
I can tell you if _____
and why _____.
Finally, I wonder whether _____

_____.

D. You have decided to look for a house. A real estate agent has just shown you a house that you like. There are many questions you want to ask him. Ask hidden questions using the following suggestions.

1. mortgage payments (I'd like to know) _____

_____

2. qualify for a mortgage (Please tell me) _____

_____

3. taxes (Would you mind telling me) _____

_____

4. downpayment (I wonder) _____

5. other costs (Can you tell me) _____

_____

6. how to offer to purchase (Please tell me) _____

_____

7. conditions of sale (Please explain) _____

_____

8. legal fees (Do you happen to know) _____

_____

9. kinds of insurance (I don't know) _____

_____

10. possession date (You didn't tell me) _____

_____

Other questions you may have:

11. _____
12. _____
13. _____
14. _____
15. _____

E. You and your family or friend are moving to another city in Canada. Your family or friend has already moved and rented an apartment or house. Write a letter asking about the accommodation. Be sure to use hidden questions. You might want to ask about rent, location, neighbors, style of house, facilities, etc.

_____

_____

_____

_____

_____

_____

_____

Unit XI

Past Progressive

A. Change the sentences in the following paragraph to the past progressive tense. (Notice the relationship between the present progressive and the past progressive.)

I am listening to the radio because the weather office is reporting that the roads are hazardous. It is a miserable day. The sun is hiding behind the dark clouds. A harsh wind is blowing and it is snowing very hard. Only a few people are walking on the slippery sidewalks. No one is driving on the icy roads.

_____
_____
_____
_____
_____
_____

B. Do you remember the last time you went to the emergency department in a hospital? List some of the things that people were doing. Make sentences using the given words. Then write your own sentences.

Example: *ambulance driver and his assistant / carry man / stretcher.*
An ambulance driver and his assistant were carrying a man on a stretcher.

1. A receptionist/ask to see/a man's health insurance card. _____

_____

2. Many people/sit/waiting room._____

_____

3. Some secretaries/type information. _____

_____

4. Someone/page/a doctor/on intercom. _____

_____

5. A pregnant woman/sit/wheelchair._____

_____

6. A mother/carry/small baby. _____

_____

7. A nurse/call out/names._____

_____

8. A little boy/hold/his father's hand. _____

_____

9. One of the nurses/take/man's blood pressure. _____

_____

10. A doctor/talk/patient. _____

_____

C. A doctor at the emergency department is asking some questions. Imagine you are the patient and answer these questions.

1. What were you doing when you first had the stomach pains? _____

_____

2. Were you eating anything unusual at dinner time? _____

_____

3. Were you doing any strenuous exercise in the afternoon? _____

_____

D. Join the following pairs of sentences to describe two activities that were happening at the same time yesterday.

Example: *The nurse was taking the patient's temperature. The doctor was writing a report.*
The nurse was taking the patient's temperature while the doctor was writing a report.

1. I was reading a magazine in the waiting room. I was waiting for my mother-in-law.

_____

_____

2. An elderly man was telling the receptionist his health insurance number. She was typing the information. _____

_____

3. An old lady was sitting in a wheelchair. Her husband was talking to the nurse.

_____

_____

4. The doctor was looking at the X-ray. I was worrying about my broken ankle.

_____

_____

E. It was 8:00 p.m. when a fire suddenly broke out in the high-rise apartment building.
a. Write the sentences below telling what the people were doing <u>when the fire started.</u>

Example: *I / do homework*
I was doing homework when the fire started.

1. The superintendent/repair/a leaky tap _____

_____

2. A young man/watch/TV _____

3. A newborn infant/sleep _____

4. A couple of girls/fry potatoes for dinner _____

_____

5. A businessman/write/report _____

_____

6. Some teenagers/listen/records _____

_____

b. Now tell what the people in (a) above did <u>when they noticed the fire</u>.

    Example: I / ring / fire alarm
                I rang the fire alarm when I noticed the fire.

1. _____

_____

2. _____

_____

3. _____

_____

4. _____

_____

5. _____

_____

6. _____

_____

F. Tell what you were doing at the time the following things occurred.

    Example: (I was writing a composition at school) when I suddenly fainted.

1. _____when someone grabbed my wallet.

2. _____when I saw the flames.

3. _____when a dog ran in front of my car.

4. _____when my car slid on the icy road.

5. _____when I saw someone enter my neighbor's window.

G. Now describe what you did when each of the above things happened.

    Example: When I suddenly fainted (someone put a cold cloth on my forehead).

1. _____

_____

2. _____

_____

3. _____

_____

4. _____

_____

5. _____

_____

H. Use the simple past or the past continuous in the following.

1. I _____ (dial) 911 when my barbecue _____ (catch) on fire.

2. The baby sitter _____ (call) the Poison Control Centre when she _____ (discover) the baby drinking paint thinner.

3. He _____ (ski) down the mountain when he _____ (trip and fall). Luckily, the ski patrol _____ (be) there to help him.

4. I _____ (call) the fire department when I _____ (notice) smoke coming out of the building.

5. While the passengers on the ship _____ (have) a good time, the ship _____ (strike) an iceberg. The passengers _____ (begin) to panic.

6. What _____ (you/do) when the fire alarm went off? I _____ (watch) my favorite quiz show on TV. What _____ (you/do) then? I _____ (put on) my coat and _____ (run)outside.

7. As the child _____ (walk) to school, a stranger _____ (approach) her. She _____ (not/speak) to him and _____ (continue) on her way.

8. While we _____ (take) a holiday in Vancouver, someone _____ (break into) our hotel room and _____ (take) all our money. I _____ (not/bring) traveller's cheques.

9. The car _____ (speed) through a red light when a police car _____ (turn) the corner. The police car _____ (stop) the speeding car. The policeman _____ (get) out and _____ (ask) the driver for his license and insurance. While the driver _____ (look) for his credentials, the policeman _____ (write) a ticket.

I. Complete the following sentences.

1. While we were camping_____

2. Just as I was opening the door _____

3. While the children were playing in the schoolground _____

_____

4. While we were celebrating our anniversary _____

_____

5. The girl was running after the ball when _____

6. When the plane landed _____

7. I was sleeping when _____

8. When my gas gauge reached empty _____

9. My friends were just leaving when _____

J. Fill in the blanks with <u>during</u> or <u>while</u>.

1. _____ he was speeding, the police caught him.

2. _____ the game, one of the players hurt his leg.

3. _____ recess, my child scraped his knee.

4. _____ the snowstorm, my car got stuck.

5. _____ we were hiking in the mountains, we saw a bear.

6. _____ I was skating, I twisted my ankle.

7. _____ his court appearance, the judge fined him $200.

8. _____ he was listening to the charges, he began to tremble.

K. Make sentences with both <u>while</u> and <u>during</u> for these situations.

Example: *We drove to Toronto. In the middle of the trip we had engine trouble.*
While we were driving to Toronto, we had engine trouble.
During our trip we had engine trouble.

1. We were attending a concert last night. In the middle of the concert, one of the musicians fainted.

a. _____

b. _____

2. My husband had a coffee break this morning. At that time he called me.

a. _____

b. _____

3. He attended high school. He studied Canadian history.

a. _____

b. _____

4. I was watching my favorite TV program. In the middle, the fire alarm rang.

a. _____

b. _____

L. Describe an accident that you or your friend might have had sometime in the past. Tell what happened at the time, what you were doing before the accident, why it happened, what you did when it happened, etc.

_____

_____

_____

_____

_____

_____

_____

_____
_____
_____
_____
_____
_____
_____
_____
_____
_____
_____

M. Imagine that you are a bank teller. A robber has just held up the bank and escaped. A police officer has arrived and is asking you several questions. Write a dialogue. Be sure to include details such as place, time, description (clothes, appearance, etc.).

_____
_____
_____
_____
_____
_____
_____
_____
_____
_____
_____
_____
_____
_____
_____
_____
_____
_____
_____

_____
_____

Unit XII

Conditional II

A. Put the verbs in brackets in the correct conditional form.

Example: I (not / drive) <u>wouldn't drive</u> if I didn't have a valid license.

1. If I (lose) _____ my license, I'd apply for a replacement.

2. If my license expired, I (renew) _____ it.

3. (be)_____ your license _____ valid if you moved here from another province?

4. (have to/I) _____ take another test if I moved here from another part of Canada?

5. Mary could use her foreign license if she (be) _____ here for only a short visit.

6. Could I drive a car if I (wear) _____ glasses?

7. What kind of identification (need/I) _____ if I applied for a license?

8. If Mary (pass) _____ her written driver's test, she could take a road test.

9. She (be able) _____ to drive if she took driving lessons.

10. I would take driving lessons if I (be) _____ you.

11. Where (get/you) _____ information about lessons if you wanted to learn to drive?

12. What (happen) _____ if I failed the test several times?

13. Where (buy/you) _____ auto insurance if you didn't have any?

14. Provided that Bob were healthy, he (can apply) _____ for a license.

15. If you were more relaxed, you (be) _____ a better driver.

B. Make the following statements into questions.

Example: If my car wouldn't start, I'd call a tow truck.
Would you call a tow truck if your car wouldn't start?
or If your car wouldn't start, would you call a tow truck?

1. If my battery were dead, I'd get a boost. _____

_____

2. We wouldn't go on vacation if we needed a new transmission. _____

_____

3. Jack wouldn't drive in the winter if he needed snow tires._____

_____

4. If my tire were flat I'd get it fixed at the garage. _____

_____

5. If you had friends in Quebec, you'd drive there. _____

_____

C. Complete these sentences using the correct form of the verb.

Example: *If I had a motorcycle,*
If I had a motorcycle, I would wear a helmet.

1. If I heard a siren while I was driving, _____

2. I would stop at a crosswalk if _____

3. If I were driving in a playground zone _____

4. If cars ran on batteries, _____

5. I wouldn't be able to drive if _____

6. We would wear seat belts if _____

7. If my car weren't safe to drive, _____

8. If my brakes weren't in good condition, _____

9. If I were looking for a new car, _____

10. Even if I could afford a Rolls Royce, _____

D. Answer the questions in complete sentence. Imagine that your friend wants to buy a car. He is asking you the following questions and would like your advice. Answer and then tell why, using conditional sentences.

Example: *Would you buy a car with a standard transmission or an automatic one?*
I'd buy a car with a standard transmission. If I bought a car with a standard transmission, I wouldn't use as much gas.

1. Would you buy a car or lease one? _____

_____

_____

2. Would you buy a used car or a new one? _____

_____

_____

3. Would you buy an American car or a foreign one? _____

_____

_____

4. Would you buy a compact car or a luxury model? _____

_____

_____

5. Would you borrow money from the bank to buy a car? _____

_____

_____

6. Would you buy a used car from a newspaper ad or from a car dealer? _____

_____

_____

7. Would you bargain on the price of the car? _____

_____

_____

8. Would you buy a car without a spare tire? _____

_____

_____

9. Would you take a car for a test run before buying it? _____

_____

_____

10. Would you take a friend with you to look at cars? _____

_____

_____

E. Give two Conditional II examples for each situation. Use the cues provided in the correct position in your sentence.

> *Example:*   *put air in the tires*
>   *a. if*   *I would put air in my tires if they were flat.*
>   *b. unless*   *I wouldn't put air in my tires unless they were flat.*

1. go to a car wash
a. unless _____
b. if _____

2. go to a self-service gas station
a. provided that _____
b. if _____

3. get a tune-up
a. unless _____
b. only if _____

4. not leave my car at home
a. if _____
b. unless _____

5. drive in winter
a. on condition that _____
b. even if _____

6. check my oil
a. on condition that _____
b. if _____

7. drive at night
a. even if _____
b. unless _____

8. pick up a hitch-hiker

a. on condition that _____

b. even if _____

9. carry a can of gasoline in my car

a. only if _____

b. even if _____

10. wear a seat belt

a. if _____

b. provided that _____

F. Decide whether the following sentences are Conditional I or II. Then, use the correct form of the verb in brackets.

Example: *The mechanic (call)* _____ *me if the car is ready.*
The mechanic will call me if the car is ready.

1. If my oil is low, (you/add) _____ some please?

2. If you trade in your car, you (not/get) _____ very much credit for it.

3. Provided that George (buy) _____ a car, he'll look for a travelling sales job.

4. I (check) _____ my car carefully if I were going on a long trip.

5. If we (go) _____ to a self-service station, will we pay less for our gas?

6. Use a credit card if you (not/have) _____ enough cash to pay for your gas.

7. If you (be) _____ sixteen years old, you can get a temporary license.

8. You cannot drive a bus unless you (pass) _____ a special test.

9. If Mary (lend) _____ her car to Bob, she would be legally responsible for him.

10. The charge (be) _____ serious if you had an accident while you were drunk.

11. Would you go to jail if the police (charge) _____ you with impaired driving?

12. If I change my tires before winter, I (feel) _____ safer.

13. (get/you) _____ a fine if a police officer stops you when you are not wearing a seat belt?

14. (hold/you) _____ a baby on your lap if you were driving?

15. I (not/buy) _____ that car unless the owner gives me a Bill of Sale.

G. Imagine that you won a free draw for a new camper-trailer. Write a composition telling where you would go, what you would do, and why. Be sure to include several Conditional II sentences.

Example: *If I won a camper-trailer, I would quit my job and take a trip from coast to coast.*

_____

_____

_____

_____

_____

_____

_____

_____

_____

_____

_____

_____

_____

_____

_____

_____

_____

_____

_____

_____

_____

H. Your friend is planning to move to Canada. After he arrives he intends to learn how to drive and then buy a car. Write a letter giving him some advice about driving lessons, getting a license, and looking for a car. Use as many Conditional II sentences as possible.

Example: *If I were you, I'd apply for a temporary license and then prepare for a road test.*

_____

_____

_____

_____

_____

_____

_____

_____

_____

_____

_____

_____

_____

_____

_____

_____

_____

Unit XIII

Past Perfect

A. Joseph took a vacation last summer. Unfortunately, someone broke into his house after he had gone away. Soon after he had discovered the burglary, he called the police. The police arrived immediately.
What did the police ask him? Make simple past perfect tense questions.

Example: ask neighbor to watch the house – leave
Had you asked a neighbor to watch the house before you left?

1. install strong locks on all your doors – leave _____

_____

2. lock all the doors – go away _____

_____

3. close all the windows – leave on your holiday _____

_____

4. turn a light on or use a timer – go on holiday _____

_____

5. stop your newspaper delivery – leave on holiday _____

_____

6. ask someone to check your mailbox – go away_____

_____

7. leave a key with a friend or neighbor – go _____

_____

8. buy homeowners' insurance – take your vacation_____

_____

9. tell someone where to reach you – leave _____

_____

10. put your valuables in a safety deposit box at the bank – take your vacation_____

_____

B. Joseph answered "yes" to some of the above questions and "no" to others. Answer the questions for Joseph.

Example: Yes, I had asked my next door neighbor to watch the house before I left.
No, I hadn't asked my neighbor to watch the house before I left.

1. _____

2. _____

3. _____

4. _____

5. _____

6. _____

7. _____

8. _____

9. _____

10. _____

C. In each of the following sentences use the simple past perfect tense to express the action that happened first, and the simple past for the action that happened close to the present time.

1. Mr. Fox _____ (talk) about his marital problems for a long time before he _____ (file) for a divorce.

2. Of course, Anna _____ (marry) her second husband only after she _____ (divorce) her first.

3. My grandfather _____ (make out) his will long before he _____ (die).

4. Legal Aid _____ (help) me find a lawyer after I _____ (ask for) assistance.

5. The judge _____ (give) the verdict at four o'clock; he _____ (listen) to the evidence first.

6. The witness _____ (swear) on a Bible before he _____ (give) his testimony.

7. He _____ (leave) a mess in his last apartment, so the landlord _____ (not/return) his damage deposit.

8. The judge _____ (dismiss) the case because the defendant _____ (not/appear).

9. Because the hit and run driver _____ (break) the law, the police _____ (be) anxious to find him.

10. Mary thinks the reason she _____ (not/get) a job was because she _____ (tell) the employer her religion.

11. The Human Rights Commission _____ (not/help) Tina since she _____ (apply) for domestic work.

12. Another employer, who _____ (go) to court for discrimination, _____ (pay) a heavy fine.

D. Combine the following sentences by using two clauses. Write a simple past perfect verb in one of the clauses and a simple past verb in the other. Work with the cues provided. Omit any unnecessary words.

Example: I arrived at 9:00. The police came at 9:20. (soon after)
Soon after I had arrived, the police came.

1a. He did not get the job last Tuesday. He went to the provincial Human Rights Commission the next day. (since) _____

_____

1b. The Human Rights Commission investigated the problem. Max filed his complaint. (after)

_____

2a. Susan lived in Saskatchewan for one year. Then her lawyer prepared a petition for divorce. (after) _____

_____

2b. The court received the petition. Later it sent her husband a petition. (as soon as)

_____

2c. Susan's husband did not reply to the petition. He did not attend the trial. (because)

_____

_____

2d. The court allowed Susan to get a divorce. Then, she received a court order that described the divorce agreement. (soon after) _____

_____

2e. Susan received the court order. Then, she applied for a Decree Absolute. (three months after) _____

_____

2f. She got the Decree Absolute. Then, she remarried. (when) _____

_____

3. Jack robbed a convenience store. That's why he went to a federal court of criminal law. (because) _____

_____

4. Frances appealed a speeding ticket. She went to a provincial court of civil law. (when)

_____

_____

5. The landlord refused to return Mike's damage deposit in July. He filed a complaint at Small Claims Court in September. (because)_____

_____

_____

6. He committed several crimes. He did this before he was thirteen years old. (by the time)

_____

_____

7. The tenant moved out of the apartment without paying his rent in March. The Small Claims Court fined him $500 in April. (since) _____

_____

_____

8. James went to Juvenile Court yesterday. He stole a bicycle last summer. (so)

_____

_____

9. The government made the laws. Then the courts administered them. (after)

_____

_____

E. Join the following sentences using the past perfect progressive in one clause and the simple past in the other.

Example: *He waited in the court room for an hour yesterday. Then he was called to the stand.*
He had been waiting in the court room for an hour yesterday when he was called to the stand.

1. He drove 60 kilometres an hour in a 30 kilometre an hour zone. Then the police charged him with speeding. _____

_____

2. He drove a stolen car. Then a police officer signaled for him to pull over to the curb.

_____

_____

3. He drove without a license for six months. Then the police caught him. _____

_____

_____

4. He gave unsupported evidence in court. Then the judge interrupted. _____

_____

_____

5. The judge listened to the evidence for a half hour. After that, he gave his verdict.

_____

_____

F. In each of the following sentences use a past perfect verb (simple or progressive) in one of the clauses and a past tense in the other.

Example: *No one (leave) left the scene of the accident until the police (come) had come.*

1. The car (hit) _____ the back of my car because he (follow) _____ too closely.

2. Even though the other driver (slam) _____ on his brakes, it was too late because he (already/collide) _____ with my car.

3. I (ask) _____ the other driver his name, address and license number after he (hit) _____ my car.

4. Several witnesses (give) _____ me their names and addresses before the police (come) _____.

5. I (call) _____ the police because the accident (cause) _____ damage over $350.

6. Since no one (be injured) _____ we (not/call) _____ an ambulance.

7. We (wait) _____ for fifteen minutes by the time the police (arrive) _____.

8. As soon as the police (arrive) _____ each of us (show) _____ them our licenses and registration. Then we each (describe) _____ the accident and (draw) _____ diagrams of what (happen) _____.

9. The driver of the other car (tell) _____ the police he (not/realize) _____ he (drive) _____ so close to my car.

10. Although the other driver (not/admit) _____ responsibility for the accident, the police (charge) _____ him with careless driving.

G. Complete the paragraph below using as many past perfect sentences as possible. Use the suggestions provided and some of your own ideas in a variety of sentence types using after, since, when, before, because, etc.

First Action	Second Action
complain	apply for Legal Aid
go in person	fill out an application form
fill out an application form	have an interview
Legal Aid investigates income and expenses	decides on legal fees
Legal Aid approves qualifications	go to a registered Legal Aid lawyer
Legal Aid is confidential	no one knows

Example: refuse to listen to his appeal   decide to go to a lawyer
When Immigration refused to listen to his appeal, Mr. Valda decided to go to a lawyer.

Mr. Valda applied for landed immigrant status but was turned down. He wanted to appeal the decision, so he decided to get legal assistance.

_____
_____
_____
_____
_____
_____
_____
_____
_____
_____

H. **Complete the paragraph below using the past perfect tense with the suggestions provided and some of your own ideas. Conclude your paragraph by telling that Mr. Chow went to his local Landlord and Tenant Advisory Board.**

First Action	*Second Action*
does not ask permission	enters Mr. Chow's apartment
is no emergency	enters the apartment
does not ask for permission	changes the locks
doesn't give ninety days notice	increases the rent
does not return the damage deposit	Mr. Chow leaves

Mr. Chow's landlord did not live up to his obligations.

_____
_____
_____
_____
_____
_____
_____
_____
_____

I. **Write a paragraph telling why Mr. Baker, a tenant, didn't live up to his obligations and was given notice to move out. Try to use as many past perfect tense sentences as possible.**

_____
_____
_____
_____
_____
_____
_____
_____
_____
_____
_____
_____
_____
_____
_____
_____
_____
_____
_____

J. Write a composition describing a situation in which you or your friend has been involved with the law. Record the sequence of events, using the past perfect tense whenever possible. If you cannot recall such a situation, read a newspaper report of a court case and describe it.

_____
_____
_____
_____
_____
_____
_____
_____
_____
_____
_____
_____
_____
_____
_____
_____
_____
_____
_____
_____
_____
_____
_____
_____
_____
_____
_____
_____
_____
_____
_____
_____
_____
_____
_____
_____

Unit XIV
Conditional III

A. Put the verb in brackets in the correct form.

Example: If Mary (rent) had rented an apartment, the monthly rent would have included property taxes.

1. If your son (not/move) _____ away from home, you could have claimed him as a deduction.

2. You (pay) _____ federal and provincial income taxes if you had worked in Canada last year.

3. If I (have) _____ a retirement plan, I would have claimed it as a deduction.

4. If you (tell) _____ me, I would have asked the daycare for a receipt.

5. If I (move) _____ to Ontario, how much sales tax would I have had to pay there?

6. You (not/pay) _____ any provincial sales tax if you had moved to Alberta.

7. Provided that you (earn) _____ more money last year, you would have paid more taxes.

8. (Hire/you) _____ an accountant, if you had owned a business?

9. If I (know) _____ that moving expenses were deductible, I would have kept the receipts.

10. What if my employer (not/give) _____ me a T4 tax slip last March?

B. Complete these questions using the correct form of the verb.

Example: If I had stayed in my country,
If I had stayed in my country, I would have paid taxes there.

1. If I had been born in Canada, _____

_____

2. Mr. Tsang would have gone to a tax clinic if _____

_____

3. You would have been happier if _____

_____

4. It would have been easier if _____

_____

5. If you hadn't reminded me about the deadline, _____

_____

6. Even if you had written Revenue Canada, _____

_____

7. If your children had been dependent, _____

_____

8. We would have complained about the error if _____

_____

9. Robert would have been in a higher tax bracket if _____

_____

C. When Henry filled out his tax form, he had several problems. Answer the questions below using the third conditional.

1. Henry's employer deducted too much money from his paycheque. What would you have done? _____

2. Henry earned interest on his savings account last year. He didn't put this on his tax form. What might he have done? _____

_____

3. Henry needed advice filling out his form. What could he have done? _____

_____

4. It was the middle of March. Henry hadn't received his T4 slips. What would you have done if you had been Henry? _____

_____

5. Henry worked part-time at a restaurant last summer. They didn't send him a T4 slip. What could he have done? _____

_____

6. He threw away the working copy of his tax form. What would you have done? _____

_____

7. Henry owed the government some money. He sent cash. What should he have done?

_____

8. Henry included his worker's compensation payments in his income tax. What would you have done? _____

_____

D. Use the third conditional to express an unreal condition in the past with a result in the present or future. Complete the following sentences.

Example: If I hadn't paid taxes this year, I would be richer now.

1. If I had been born sixty-five years ago, _____

2. If we hadn't come to Canada, _____

3. If taxes hadn't gone up, _____

4. If I had learned English as a child, _____

5. If Bob had got a refund, _____

6. If I had completed the form without help, _____

E. Decide whether the following sentences are conditional I, II, III or mixed. Use the correct form of the verb in brackets. Watch for negative and interrogative sentences.

Example: If I (return) <u>had returned</u> the form in May, it would have been late.

1. Do you have to pay sales tax if you (buy) _____ a new car?

2. If I lived in Quebec, on what goods (be/there) _____ sales tax?

3. How could I find out the property tax if I (think) _____ about buying a house?

4. If taxes are going up, where (go/all the money) _____?

5. If I had received a notice of assessment, (include/it) _____ both my provincial and federal tax?

6. Could I pay my taxes in instalments if I (want) _____?

7. If I had overpaid, (receive/I) _____ interest on my credit?

8. Where would I write if I (have) _____ a problem with my tax form?

9. Hung could have completed his form in French if he (be unable to read) _____ English.

10. If I (be) _____ an accountant, I could fill out the form easily.

11. Would my wife have had to fill out a form if she (not work) _____ last year?

12. If I had received Family Allowance payments last year, (have to/I) _____ include them as income this year?

13. If you are filling out your form, remember the taxation year (be) _____ the same as the calendar year.

14. On condition that your business has some income, you (can claim) _____ the business expenses.

F. Complete the following sentences using the correct form.

1. If I were a millionaire, _____

2. We'll stay in Canada if _____

3. I'd be happier if _____

4. My friend won't come to Canada if _____

5. If I get a raise, _____

6. If you had stayed up late working on your tax return, _____
_____

7. If I had wanted to pay my tax in instalments, _____
_____

8. We would pay higher taxes if _____

9. Keep all the information slips you receive if _____
_____

G. Your friend was offered a job in your country last year. He didn't accept the offer but often wonders what his life would have been like if he had gone there. He wants you to tell him about the tax system there and how he would have been taxed if he had moved to your country. **Using conditional III sentences wherever possible, write a composition telling him whether there is a sales tax, what things he would have paid tax for, what kind of taxes he would have paid, how much of his income would have gone to taxes, where the money would have gone, how taxes are collected, etc.**

H. **Write a composition describing how your life would have been different if you hadn't come to Canada and either stayed in your own country or chosen another country to live in. Discuss work, activities and daily routine, customs and habits, housing, holidays, etc. Use conditional III sentences as often as possible.**

Unit XV

Wish

A. Put the verb in brackets in the correct form.

Example: I wish my sister (be) were here, but she isn't.

1. We wish we (take) _____ the train instead of the bus to Toronto last summer.
2. I wish there (be) _____ a direct flight to Saskatoon, but there isn't.
3. My suitcase got lost. I wish I (only/take) _____ hand luggage.
4. Mikhail didn't buy cancellation insurance. He wishes he (buy) _____ some.
5. Hiroko left her carry-on case in the departure lounge. She wishes she (not/forget) _____ it.
6. Ann wants to fly to Halifax. Ann wishes the airlines (not/be) _____ on strike.
7. The stewardess doesn't speak Japanese. Toshi wishes she (speak) _____ Japanese.
8. The flight arrived early. Lam wishes he (check) _____ the flight schedule.
9. Are you sure you won't be able to drive me to the airport? I wish you (change) _____ your mind.
10. I wish I (be) _____ in my native country right now.

B. Complete the following sentences.

Example: Jack is late because he didn't take a bus to school.
He wishes <u>he had taken a bus to school.</u>

1. He forgot to get a transfer. Now he has to pay again. He wishes he _____
_____

2. You missed your stop. You have to walk six blocks. You wish you _____
_____

3. I don't have the exact fare. I have to get change. I wish _____
_____

4. The taxi ride was expensive. I'm broke. I wish I _____
_____

5. I didn't buy a bus pass. I'd save money if I had one. I wish I _____
_____

6. It's 1:00 a.m. The number fifteen bus doesn't run after midnight. Now I have to take a taxi or walk. I wish _____
_____

7. Monica didn't know she could get a school bus pass. She'd pay less if she had one. She wishes _____

8. Giorgio can't meet me at the station. I wish he _____
_____

9. I missed the express bus. I wish I _____
_____

10. I'm too tired to walk home. I wish I _____
_____

C. Answer the following questions with a negative statement and then an affirmative statement using <u>wish</u>.

Example: *Did you see the ticket agent?*
                   No, I didn't. I wish I had.

1. Are you taking a holiday this summer?_____

2. Were you in Mexico last winter? _____

3. Can you get a visa by next week? _____

4. Are you going to take a package tour?_____

5. Was there room for you on stand-by?_____
_____

6. Is it cheap to travel first class? _____

7. Will someone meet you at the airport? _____
_____

8. Did Bob find his luggage claim? _____

9. Do you know which platform the train leaves from? _____
_____

10. Can you rest comfortably on a bus? _____

D. Last summer you went to Montreal. You have some regrets about the trip. comment on the following situations using <u>wish</u>.

Example: *more time in Montreal*
                   I wish I had spent more time in Montreal last summer.

1. some souvenirs _____

2. travellers' cheques _____

3. so much rich food _____

4. a good map of the city _____

5. so many suitcases _____

6. a reservation _____

7. lighter clothes _____

8. a guide _____

9. speak French _____

10. Quebec city also _____

E. Make a statement using <u>wish</u> for the following.

1. Mary has just caught the one o'clock bus to Winnipeg. The bus driver is telling her that the eleven o'clock bus was the only express bus. _____
_____

2. You're sick in bed with the flu. You can't go camping this weekend. _____
_____

3. Tom came late. The train has just left the platform. _____
_____

4. You took a small plane. You don't like travelling in small planes. _____
_____

5. Minh took a bus. There were no seats because it was rush hour. _____
_____

6. You took the plane to Kamloops. The train is cheaper and you would have seen the Rocky Mountains. _____
_____

7. Luu walked to the hotel. It took two hours. _____
_____

8. The man sitting beside you is talkative. You want to read your book. _____
_____

9. Daniel fell asleep during the flight. He didn't see the Great Lakes._____
_____

10. You get car-sick. You're travelling to Toronto by car. _____
_____

F. Use <u>hope</u> or <u>wish</u> to fill in the blanks.

1. I _____ I can see the Laurentians next summer.

2. My brother _____ he liked sea travel, but he doesn't.

3. I _____ the plane comes soon.

4. I _____ you visited me more often.

5. They _____ the flight arrives on time.

6. Anna _____ to buy some souvenirs on her vacation.

7. We _____ the customs inspector doesn't check our bags.

8. I _____ the stewardess will help my mother board the plane.

9. Hong _____ he had bought an economy class ticket, but he didn't.

10. I _____ you would rent a car so we could travel around the southern part of the province this weekend.

11. I _____ I had a bicycle, but I don't.

12. We _____ to take a ferry boat to Victoria if we can.

G. Write a composition telling about a trip you took in which everything went wrong. You regret many of the events during the trip. Make sentences with <u>wish</u> to present your ideas. The following may be helpful: you didn't use a travel agent; your transportation plans failed; you got the wrong kind of ticket; you ate at terrible restaurants and stayed in poor accommodation; you didn't visit the most interesting places. What do you hope to do to make your next trip more enjoyable?

_____
_____
_____
_____
_____
_____
_____
_____
_____
_____
_____
_____
_____
_____
_____
_____

H. Write a composition telling where you wish you could go on your vacation. Tell why, what you wish you could do, etc.

_____
_____
_____
_____
_____
_____
_____
_____
_____
_____
_____
_____
_____
_____
_____
_____

I. Write a composition telling that you wish certain things here were more like they were in your country. (e.g., transportation, food, housing, clothing, language, entertainment)

_____
_____
_____
_____
_____
_____
_____
_____
_____
_____
_____
_____
_____
_____
_____
_____
_____
_____
_____
_____
_____
_____
_____
_____
_____
_____
_____
_____
_____
_____
_____
_____

Unit XVI

Joining Words

I. *Using Joining Words to Express Cause and Effect Relationships*

A. Join the following sentences in two ways. Vary the position of the independent clause. Notice the punctuation.

Example: *I want to find a new job. I should prepare a personal résumé.*
Because/Since/As I want to find a new job, I should prepare a persoanl résumé.
or   I should prepare a personal résumé because/since/as I want to find a new job.

1. There are job openings. Employees retire, transfer or are fired. _____
_____
_____

2. New jobs are not always advertised in newspapers. You should tell other people what you are looking for. _____
_____
_____

3. There are new positions. Businesses open and others expand. _____
_____
_____

4. You should meet employers in person. They like to judge an applicant's suitability for the job. _____
_____
_____

5. Find out who hires employees where you are looking for work. You might waste time speaking to the wrong people. _____
_____
_____

6. Be prepared to answer questions. The employer will want to know all about you. _____
_____
_____

7. Be ready to ask intelligent questions about the place of employment. Employers like to know you are interested in their company. _____
_____
_____

B. Complete the following sentences. Punctuate correctly.

1. I did not apply for the job because _____
_____

2. As my friend knows about an opening in her office _____
_____

3. My friend went to an employment agency since _____
_____

4. I'm looking for a job as a _____ because _____
_____

5. Since my friend is a certified electrician _____
_____

6. I don't want to transfer to another city because _____
_____

7. Gunther was laid off since _____
_____

8. I don't want to work as a _____ since _____
_____

C. Use the ideas in brackets to complete the following sentences. Punctuate correctly.

Example: *(my résumé was well written)*
Because of my well-written résumé, the employer called me to come for an interview.

1. (I had training for the job) Because of _____
_____I was well qualified.

2. (I was experienced in the field) Due to_____
_____the boss offered me a good starting salary.

3. (I was nervous) Due to the fact that_____
_____I couldn't sleep the night before my interview.

4. (The traffic is heavy during rush hour) Due to _____
_____I left my house early.

5. (The office was pleasant and the employer was friendly) Because of_____
_____I felt relaxed and confident.

D. Complete the following sentences telling about one's suitability for various kinds of work. Use transitional expressions. Punctuate correctly.

Example: *I can't type; consequently, / therefore, I can't get a job as a secretary.*

1. I go to school during the day; _____
_____

2. I do not drive a car;_____
_____

3. My friend is an experienced mechanic; _____

_____

4. You are not interested in manual labor; _____

_____

5. Robert has a chauffeur's license;_____

_____

6. Luisa speaks four languages and she has excellent office skills; _____

_____

7. I like working with children; _____

_____

8. Your word processing skills are rusty;_____

_____

E. Combine the following sentences by using <u>so...that</u> or <u>such...that</u>.

Example: The company is progressive. It has attracted top-notch employees.
The company is <u>so</u> progressive <u>that</u> it has attracted top-notch employees.

1. The job is boring. I think I'll look for a better position. _____

_____

2. The salary was low. I decided to quit. _____

_____

3. I felt sick. I couldn't go to work. _____

_____

4. He is a helpful foreman. I enjoy working with him. _____

_____

5. This is a busy office. There is always a lot of work to do. _____

_____

F. Use <u>so (such)...that</u> to expand these ideas into sentences.

Example: He is careless.
He is <u>so</u> careless <u>that</u> he never does his job well.

1. Your boss speaks too quickly. _____

_____

2. The work was easy. _____

_____

3. The factory is spotless. _____

_____

4. It is an excellent opportunity. _____

_____

5. Your colleague was tired. _____

_____

G. Use the following in complete sentences.

Example: so challenging that
The job was so challenging that I learned many new things.

1. so interesting that _____

_____

2. so much money that _____

_____

3. so many hours that _____

_____

4. so difficult that _____

_____

5. so few benefits that _____

_____

6. so close to home that _____

_____

7. so early that _____

_____

8. so tired that _____

_____

H. Use the following in complete sentences.

1. such a good interview that _____

_____

2. such important questions that _____

_____

3. such a kind employer that _____

_____

4. such poor training that _____

_____

5. such helpful people that _____

_____

6. such a good opportunity that _____

_____

7. such a lot of work to do that _____

_____

8. such low wages that _____

_____

I. In the following use the given joining words to combine the two sentences provided. Punctuate correctly and be prepared to explain the meaning of your new sentence.

Example: You went to the office. You had a job interview.
<u>You went to the office</u> because <u>you had a job interview</u>.

You couldn't go to work. You had a high fever.

_____consequently _____

_____

Due to _____

_____

Since _____

_____

_____such_____that _____

_____

Because of_____

_____

As _____

_____

Lee got a big raise. She bought a new car.

_____such_____that _____

_____

_____as _____

_____

_____therefore_____

_____

_____as a result_____

_____

Due to _____

_____

Because_____

_____

II. Using Joining Words to Express Purpose.

A. Combine these sentences. Use <u>so (that)</u>.

Example: I'm going to skip my coffee break. I want to finish my work.
I'm going to skip my coffee break so (that) I can finish my work.

1. I cashed my pay cheque yesterday. I wanted to have enough money for the weekend.

_____

_____

2. I bought a car. I wanted to work as a travelling salesman. _____
_____

3. Jack is taking accounting at night school. He wants to advance in his job.
_____
_____

4. You wore a clean suit to the interview. You wanted to make a good impression on the
personnel manager. _____
_____

5. Did you find out about the job and the employer? You want to discuss the work
intelligently._____
_____

B. Complete these sentences.

1. You wrote a résumé so (that) _____

2. Your résumé was short and well organized so (that) _____
_____

3. It is important to write about your skills and accomplishments so (that)_____
_____

4. You should ask previous employers for a reference so (that) _____
_____

5. Be sure to include your phone number and address so (that) _____
_____

C. Fill in the blanks with <u>so</u> (for relationships of cause and effect) or <u>so that</u> (for relationships of purpose). If both are possible, be prepared to explain the differences in meaning. Punctuate.

1. I'll upgrade my skills _____ I can get a better job.

2. My family is moving to the United States _____ I'll have to quit my job.

3. Our office was over-crowded _____ we moved to a larger one.

4. Bob was transferred to Toronto by his company _____ they will pay for his moving expenses.

5. My boss allowed me to take time off _____ I could go to the dentist.

6. Business is very good _____ my company is going to hire two more employees.

7. Jean took a computer course _____ she could operate the computer at work.

8. Tan's boss is pleased with his performance _____ he plans to give Tan a raise.

9. Mary is taking education at university _____ she can become a high school teacher.

10. Linda loves animals _____ she would like to be a veterinarian when she grows up.

D. Join the following sentences with <u>in order to</u>, or <u>to</u>.

Example: He got a Social Insurance Number. He had to have proof of identity.
He got a Social Insurance Number <u>in order to / to</u> have proof of identity.

1. You worked overtime. You wanted to earn time-and-a-half. _____

_____

2. Did you work on Labor Day? Do you want to take time off at a later date? _____

_____

3. We pay employment insurance each month. We want to receive benefits if we lose our jobs.

_____

_____

4. I reported the accident to my foreman. I wanted to make a claim._____

_____

5. John is apprenticing as an electrician. He wants to get his license _____

_____

_____

6. Sylvie made an appointment to see her boss. She wants to ask for maternity leave. _____

_____

III. *Using Joining Words to Express Relationships of Contrast (Unexpected Results).*

A. Complete the following sentences using correct punctuation.

Example: Even though / Although   he is eighteen years old, his employer
doesn't pay him the minimum wage.
His employer doesn't pay him the minimum wage <u>even though / although</u>
he is eighteen years old.

1. Even though he works more than eight hours a day _____

_____

2. Although his boss did not give him notice of termination of employment _____

_____

3. _____
although she hasn't had a raise in five years.

4. _____
even though she has worked in that factory for twelve consecutive months.

B. Write sentences using <u>in spite of</u> or <u>despite</u> for the following.

Example: Even though Henri had a flat tire, he arrived at the interview on time.
<u>Despite / In spite of</u> (having) a flat tire, Henri arrived at the interview on
time.

1. Even though he was nervous, he spoke with confidence. _____

_____

2. Although he knew a lot about the company, he asked several questions at the interview.

_____

3. Although Lan speaks English poorly, he went to the interview alone. _____

_____

4. Even though the boss asked him some technical questions, Josef was able to answer them without difficulty. _____

_____

5. There was a long line of applicants but the boss didn't rush Maribel._____

_____

C. Change the following sentences by using <u>nonetheless</u>, <u>nevertheless</u> or <u>however</u>.

Example: *She felt ill, but she went to work anyway.*
She felt ill; <u>however, /nonetheless, /nevertheless,</u> she went to work.

1. The salary was low, but Mary accepted the job anyway._____

_____

2. Although Martin worked nine hours a day, they never paid him for overtime. _____

_____

3. Georgio was a member of the union, but he did not go on strike. _____

_____

4. Even though I have professional training from another country, I had to get my qualifications approved. _____

_____

5. Although I would like to work in industry, I'll accept this job because the experience will be good for me. _____

_____

D. Write as many sentences as you can using <u>on the other hand</u> or <u>whereas</u> to contrast working conditions in Canada with those in your country.

Example: *In Canada men do a large proportion of the manual labor; <u>on the other hand/whereas</u> most of the manual labor is done by women in my country.*

_____
_____
_____
_____
_____
_____
_____
_____
_____
_____

IV. *Using Joining Words in Relationships of Sequence and Addition of Information.*

A. Write a paragraph to explain the necessary steps in hunting for a job. Include sequence adverbs and those used for adding information.

1. Decide what kind of job you are looking for.
2. Look in the newspaper and yellow pages of the phone book.
3. Talk to friends about possible openings.
4. Go to employment agencies.
5. Write a résumé.
6. Find references.
7. Write a cover letter.
8. Contact possible employers and arrange for an interview.
9. Fill out application forms.
10. Prepare for the interview.

_____
_____
_____
_____
_____
_____
_____
_____
_____
_____
_____
_____
_____
_____
_____
_____
_____
_____

B. For each of the following classified ads write sentences about your suitability and interest in the job. Use the joining words that are provided. Remember to use correct punctuation.

Telephone Canvasser. Full time. Good command of spoken English. Out of town; own transportation nec. $6.00 per hr. plus commission. Apply in person 10-12 a.m.

Example: As _____

As I do not own a car, this job is not suitable for me.

1. _____ therefore _____

_____

2. Since _____

_____

3. Although _____

_____

4. _____because _____

_____

5. _____however _____

_____

6. _____so _____

_____

7. _____in order to _____

_____

8. _____so_____that

_____

Courier: Drivers/owners req'd by local courier company. Flexible hours. Must have newer model car. Experience an asset.

1. Even though _____

_____

2. _____since _____

_____

3. _____such_____that

_____

4. Due to_____

_____

5. _____to _____

_____

6. Despite the fact that_____

_____

7. _____as a result _____

_____

8. _____in addition_____

_____

Receptionist: Part-time receptionist req'd for D.T. company. Evenings and alternate Saturdays. Typing and some office experience necessary. Competitive salary.

1. _____because _____

_____

2. _____so_____

_____

3. _____on the other hand _____

_____

4. Due to the fact that_____

_____

5. Although _____

_____

6. _____ however _____

_____

7. _____ moreover _____

_____

8. _____ in brief _____

_____

C. **Use the ideas <u>to be well</u> (or <u>not be well</u>) + <u>to go to work</u> (or <u>not got to work</u>). Punctuate correctly. Be prepared to explain the meaning of your sentence.**

Example: *Because I was not well this morning*
                  Because I was not well this morning, I did not go to work.

1. I went to work even though _____

2. Although I was well this morning _____

3. I was not well this morning; therefore _____

4. I was not well this morning; nevertheless _____

5. I was so ill this morning that _____

6. I was well this morning so _____

7. I did not go to work this morning since _____

8. In spite of _____ I went to work this morning.

9. Because of _____ I did not go to work.

D. **Write a composition using as many joining words as possible to compare and contrast employment for your particular work in your country with that in Canada**
     or
     Write a composition using as many joining words as possible to discuss the following aspects regarding work in Canada or work in your country only. Here are some suggestions for the above topics. Choose no more than three of these areas to develop your composition.

Finding job openings; How to apply for a job; The interview; Employer-employee relationships; Working conditions (work hours, breaks, overtime, salary, benefits, working environment.)

_____

_____

_____

_____

_____

_____

_____

_____

_____
_____
_____
_____
_____
_____
_____
_____
_____
_____
_____
_____
_____
_____
_____
_____
_____
_____
_____
_____
_____
_____
_____
_____
_____

E. A Typical Pay Stub (teachers may want to review the elements of information in this stub).

United Automotives Limited
65 Fairchild Road
Calgary, Alberta T6N 5H4

000001502
SIN 706-596-201

Rate	Hrs./Units	Amount	Deductions		Year-to-Date	
10.15	80	815.63	CPP	13.48	Gross Pay	15640.15
			EI	12.51	CPP	259.93
			Income Tax	140.69	Co. Pension	
			Union Dues	9.00	EI	212.70
					Income Tax	2882.71
Total Earnings		815.63	Total Deductions	175.68	Net Pay	639.95

Name:	LAM, Nhung	Ident.: E930 2760 59345

Statement of Earnings and Deductions	Period Ending Date:	11-15-96

F. With your teacher's guidance, write a personal résumé. Be sure to include the information provided in the résumé notes on the next two pages.

_____
_____
_____
_____
_____
_____
_____
_____
_____
_____
_____
_____
_____
_____
_____
_____
_____
_____
_____

G. Choose an advertisement from the classified section of the newspaper and write a letter of application to accompany your résumé using the model in the following pages.

_____
_____
_____
_____
_____
_____
_____
_____
_____
_____
_____
_____
_____
_____
_____
_____
_____
_____
_____

Sample Application Form

Permanent ○   Temporary ○   Part-time ○

Position Sought:_____

Availability Date: _____

Preferred Employment Locations (cities): _____

_____

General Information

Last name:_____ First Name:_____

Address: _____

_____

_____

Driver's Licence: ○ Yes   ○ No   Class: _____

Do you speak or write French?   ○ No   ○ A little   ○ Well   ○ Fluently

Other languages:_____

Are you legally eligible to accept employment in Canada?   ○ Yes   ○ No
(You may be requested to provide proof if a job offer is made)

Education

Enter the names of all educational institutions attended, beginning with the most recent. Indicate your major (subject studied), and dates attended (month/year), the degree or diploma and date it was obtained (or if in progress, date you expect to obtain it).

_____

_____

_____

_____

_____

_____

_____

_____

_____

_____

_____

Work Experience

Please list all employment starting with the most recent.

Employer, Address and Phone Number: _____

_____

_____

Dates employed: _____

Job Title and Description: _____

_____

_____

Immediate Supervisor:_____

Employer, Address and Phone Number: _____

_____

_____

Dates Employed: _____

Job Title and Description:_____

_____

_____

Immediate Supervisor: _____

Employer, Address and Phone Number: _____

_____

_____

Dates Employed: _____

Job Title and Description:_____

_____

_____

Immediate Supervisor: _____

Activities

Indicate your extra-curricular activities, memberships in clubs and organizations, leadership roles, sports activities, hobbies, etc.

_____

_____

_____

_____

_____

_____

_____

_____

Résumé Notes

Personal Information: Include name, address, telephone number, social insurance number

Education: Be sure to include courses studied, certificates, diplomas and awards received.

Work Experience:
1. Include summer, part-time, temporary and full time experience.
2. Provide the title of your position and what jobs you performed.
3. Tell what kind of job you are now interested in.

Activities:
1. List clubs and organizations to which you belong and whether you hold an office in any of them.
2. Include hobbies and sports.

References: Provide three references. Never use a relative and try to avoid using a minister.
Always ask a person for permission to use his or her name as a reference.

Sample Résumé
Name
Address
City, Province, Postal Code
Phone (you can also include fax, cell phone, e-mail)
Social Insurance Number

Educational History

Post Secondary
(dates; institution; degree, diploma or certificate obtained)

High School
(graduation date; name of school)

Special Courses
(dates; length of course; where course offered; certificate obtained – these should be courses which may have some value in the type of employment you are seeking).

Work Experience

Starting with your most recent employment, list the names of your employers, the dates you worked for them, your job title, duties performed or skills acquired, and the name of your immediate supervisor.

Activities

List any extracurricular activities you participate in, particularly those in which you hold/have held leadership positions or have acquired team skills. Include organizations/clubs you belong to (past or present), sports, hobbies, etc.

References

Give the names of three people who can provide a reference for you. Job references are the most useful, followed by references from teachers, volunteer supervisors, or anyone who has been in a position to assess your work and leadership skills and your character. Character references alone are of minimal use in job applications. Include the name, position, address and phone number of each of your references, and be sure to ask the person's permission to use them as a reference.

Other Information

Add any other information that could tell potential employers about your work skills, your education, your leadership skills, your character, etc., which could not be covered under the above. Be specific.

Résumé Formats

Résumé formats can vary widely, depending on what type of information you wish to highlight, or what type of employment you are seeking. Consult books in your local library on seeking employment or talk to someone at your local Canada Employment Centre for more information.

Sample Letter of Application (Cover Letter)

69 Windsor Drive,
Calgary, Alberta T5E 4H6

November 19, 1999

Mr. C.S. Smart, President
King Manufacturing Limited,
3020 Industrial Road,
Red Deer, Alberta T7A 2B8

Dear Mr. Smart:

I have read your ad in the November 18 issue of the Calgary *Herald* and am interested in applying for the position of shipping supervisor. If the position is still open, I would appreciate your considering me for the job.

Since leaving high school in 1991, I have had responsible experience in the field.

Please find the enclosed résumé of my qualifications. I would be happy to meet with you for a personal interview at your convenience.

Sincerely,

Jack Patterson

Letter of Application Notes

1. Use good quality 8 1/2 x 11 inch white paper.

2. Do not use letterhead paper.

3. Try to address the person to whom you are writing, rather than using "Dear Sir or Madam."

4. Form:
    a. Opening Paragraph: Tell why you are writing, how you know about the position and exactly what kind of job you are interested in.
    b. Middle Paragraph: Give your reason for wanting this type of work. Mention any relevant experience you have had.
    c. Closing Paragraph: State your willingness to come for an interview.

Unit XVII

The Passive Voice

A. Change the following passive sentences to active voice.

1. The B.N.A. Act was written by the Fathers of Confederation. _____

_____

2. The law will be passed in the House of Commons next week. _____

_____

3. The Bill will be passed by the Federal Government. _____

_____

4. The Bill is prepared by the Minister. _____

5. A Bill must be approved by the Cabinet. _____

6. A lot of work is done by parliamentary committees. _____

_____

7. M.P.s are elected by citizens. _____

8. Laws can be changed by the Canadian Government without Britain's approval. _____

_____

B. Change the following sentences from active to passive. Be sure to use the same tense that is used in the original sentence. Use <u>by</u>-phrases only if necessary.

Example: *A Prime Minister leads the Government of Canada.*
      The Government of Canada is led by a Prime Minister.

1. The judge questioned the applicant about Canadian history. _____

_____

2. The judge has approved Maria's application for citizenship. _____

_____

3. Applicants always submit documents. _____

_____

4. The new Canadians have taken oaths of citizenship. _____

_____

5. All Canadians must obey the laws of the country. _____

_____

6. Canadians respect freedom of speech. _____

_____

7. The judge asked Sonia about the Canadian system of government. _____

_____

_____

8. The Canadian people elect the Members of Parliament. _____

_____

9. The Governor General has just appointed a new senator to the Senate. _____

_____

_____

10. The leader of the largest party form the Government. _____

_____

11. The party with the most elected Members of Parliament will govern the country. _____

_____

_____

12. The Opposition is going to examine the Government's actions. _____

_____

13. The Prime Minister is choosing a new Cabinet. _____

_____

14. The Prime Minister and Cabinet make government policies. _____

_____

C. Change the following active sentences to passive if possible. Include the by-phrase only if it is necessary. If the sentence cannot be changed be prepared to explain why.

1. You came here last month. _____

2. My husband has filled out this application for citizenship. _____

_____

3. The English Parliament passed the B.N.A. Act in 1867. _____

_____

4. The B.N.A. Act united the colonies of Nova Scotia, New Brunswick and Canada (Ontario and Quebec). _____

_____

5. The Parliament of Canada created the Yukon as a separate territory in 1898. _____

_____

6. In 1947 the Government passed the Canadian Citizenship Act. _____

_____

7. Canadians adopted a Canadian flag in 1965. _____

_____

8. The Governor General represents the Queen. _____

_____

9. Queen Elizabeth II signed the new Constitution on April 17, 1982. _____

_____

10. The Constitution gives Canada a new Charter of Rights. _____

_____

11. The Governor General does not govern the country. _____

_____

12. Someone announced the results of the election. _____

_____

13. The opposition party has been examining the Government's actions. _____

_____

14. The reporter gave the results of the election. _____

_____

15. M.P.s often go to their constituencies. _____

_____

D. Change the following sentences which contain modals to the passive voice. Use a <u>by</u>-phrase only if necessary.

1. They must hold an election every five years. _____

_____

2. We should elect good representatives. _____

_____

3. The House of Commons couldn't pass the law. _____

_____

4. The House of Commons may debate that question today. _____

_____

5. All citizens should respect the law. _____

_____

6. Someone who is a security risk cannot receive citizenship. _____

_____

7. The Government might not give citizenship to a criminal. _____

_____

8. You must provide two recent photographs. _____

_____

9. Each adult has to pay $15.00. _____

_____

E. The following sentences are written in the passive voice without agents. Rewrite each sentence, using the correct form of the verb. Consider the time expression given.

Example: The question (debate) now.
The question is being debated now.

1. Our Prime Minister (know) throughout the world. _____

_____

2. The Parliament buildings (tour) every day. _____

_____

3. On April 17, 1982, the Canadian people (give) a new Charter of Rights. _____

_____

4. A protest march (hold) next week. _____

_____

5. Membership in certain professions (sometime/restrict) to Canadian citizens. _____

_____

6. The money which (donate) last week will help the poor._____

_____

7. His political activities (investigate) when he left Canada illegally. _____

_____

8. The campaign (hold) for a month before the election. _____

_____

9. Canada (make up of) ten provinces and three territories. _____

_____

10. A new Prime Minister (elect) in the next Federal election? _____

_____

11. Senators (elect) to office?_____

_____

12. (call) When the next election? _____

_____

F. Write a composition describing how elections take place in your country, or here in Canada. Use as many passive constructions as possible.

_____
_____
_____
_____
_____
_____
_____
_____
_____
_____
_____
_____
_____
_____
_____
_____
_____
_____

G. Write a composition explaining the steps one must take in applying for Canadian citizenship. Again, use as many passive constructions as possible.

Unit XVIII

Causative Verbs

A. Change the following sentences from active to passive.

Example: *Jack had someone wash his car.*
Jack had his car washed.

1. Bob had someone take his photograph. _____

2. Paula had someone clean her rugs. _____

3. Do you always get someone to cut your grass? _____
_____

4. Bob didn't have anyone repair his flat tire. _____
_____

5. Maria will get someone to look after her child. _____
_____

6. Thu had someone send flowers to her sick aunt. _____
_____

7. Olga got someone to develop her pictures of her summer holiday. _____
_____

8. Max forgot to get someone to connect his phone. _____
_____

9. Joseph got someone to change his snow tires. _____
_____

10. Did George get anyone to fix his watch? _____

B. Make a question and then answer with <u>get</u> in both the passive and active voices.

Example: *hair / cut / **Beautiful You** (hairdresser).*
Who can I get to cut my hair? / Where can I get my hair cut?
*You can get a hairdresser at **Beautiful You** to cut your hair. / You can get it cut at **Beautiful You**.*

1. brakes/check/*Speedy Brake* (a mechanic)

Q. _____
A1. _____
A2. _____

2. house/insure/*All Care Insurance* (an insurance agent).

Q. _____
A1. _____
A2. _____

3. car/paint/*Rainbow Paints* (an auto painter)

Q. _____

A1. _____

A2. _____

4. furnace/clean/*Best Furnaces* (a heating expert)

Q. _____

A1. _____

A2. _____

5. flowers/deliver (from)/*Flower Heaven* (the florist)

Q. _____

A1. _____

A2. _____

6. curtains/make/a drapery store (a seamstress)

Q. _____

A1. _____

A2. _____

7. skates/sharpen/*ABC* (an employee)

Q. _____

A1. _____

A2. _____

8. oil/change/the corner gas station (an attendant)

Q. _____

A1. _____

A2. _____

9. pizza/deliver (from)/Tony's Pizza (a delivery boy)

Q. _____

A1. _____

A2. _____

10. washing machine/service/Canada Appliance (a serviceman)

Q. _____

A1. _____

A2. _____

C. Use <u>have</u> and <u>get</u> to change these sentences from passive to active.

Example: *He got his tooth filled. (the dentist)*
He got the dentist to fill his tooth.
He had the dentist fill his tooth.

1. You got your sofa delivered. (the furniture store)

_____

_____

2. Mary had the letter typed. (her secretary)

_____

_____

3. Did you have your broken chair replaced? (the store)

_____

_____

4. The musician got his piano tuned. (the piano tuner)

_____

_____

5. Did you get your house cleaned? (a cleaning lady)

_____

_____

6. I got the dripping tap repaired. (the plumber)

_____

_____

7. We had our broken antenna fixed. (the TV repairman)

_____

_____

8. Did you get your eyes examined? (the optometrist)

_____

_____

9. Mr. Chan got his roof retiled. (the roofer)

_____

_____

10. I had a carpet installed. (the carpet layer)

_____

_____

11. My mother didn't get the lock changed. (the locksmith)

_____

_____

D. What should you do in the following situations? Use a passive causative pattern in your answer with <u>get</u> or <u>have</u>.

Example: _My dog hurt its leg._
You should have your dog's leg examined.

1. Your roof is leaking. _____

2. Your house needs painting. _____

3. The heel on your shoe is broken. _____

4. You want more cupboards in your kitchen. _____

_____

5. There are lots of weeds in your lawn. _____

_____

6. Your house is very cold. Your furnace is out of order. _____

_____

7. Your hair is long and messy. _____

8. Your white jacket is very dirty. _____

9. You lost your key. You want another one. _____

_____

10. There is something wrong with your oven. _____

_____

E. When you go on holiday, you always ask your friend or neighbor to look after your house while you are away. Write a paragraph telling some of the things you get (have) your friend or neighbor to do (do) for you.

_____
_____
_____
_____
_____
_____
_____
_____
_____
_____
_____
_____
_____
_____

F. Choose one of the following topics and write a paragraph.

a. Mary felt like a change, so she went to the beauty shop. Her husband didn't recognize her when she got home. Why? Tell what things she had (or got) done.

b. Your car needed servicing before winter. You took it to a mechanic. Tell what things you had (or got) done.

_____
_____
_____
_____
_____
_____
_____
_____
_____
_____
_____

G. Prepare a list of ten things your teachers <u>made</u> you do when you were a child. Then, tell what your teacher(s) <u>make</u> or <u>don't make</u> you do here.

1. _____
2. _____
3. _____
4. _____
5. _____
6. _____
7. _____
8. _____
9. _____
10. _____

H. Complete the following sentences using <u>make</u> plus an adjective or <u>make</u> plus a verb.

Example: The joke in the magazine made me laugh.

1. Cold weather makes me _____ because _____

2. Poorly behaved children make me _____

3. The movie made me _____ because _____

4. The smell coming from the bakery made me _____

5. The news that _____ made me _____

Ia. List ten things permissive parents let their child do.

1. _____
2. _____
3. _____
4. _____
5. _____
6. _____
7. _____
8. _____
9. _____
10. _____

Ib. Write a short composition telling what you would and wouldn't let your children do.

_____

_____

_____

_____
_____
_____
_____
_____
_____
_____
_____
_____
_____
_____
_____

J. Use <u>help</u> in two ways to tell if you help someone in your household (e.g., spouse, parent) do (to do) various jobs. Use the suggestions given, then add your own.

Example: wash the floors
I help my wife wash the floors. I help my wife to wash the floors.

1. do the laundry _____

2. clean the garage _____

3. vacuum the carpets _____

4. weed the garden _____

5. iron the clothes _____

6. _____

7. _____

8. _____

K. Comment on the following situations. Use the given cues.

Example: I moved into a new apartment. (my cousin / help)
My cousin helped me move into a new apartment.
or   My cousin helped me to move into a new apartment.

1. I had to iron the clothes. (my mother/make) _____
_____

2. My brother defrosted the fridge. (I/get) _____
_____

3. Susan went to a party. (her mother/let) _____
_____

4. The plumber installed my sink. (I/have) _____
_____

5. Juan unpacked boxes. (the boss/make) _____
_____

6. I go home early on weekends. (my boss/let) _____

_____

7. I did the laundry. (my sister/help) _____

_____

8. The carpenter built some shelves. (I/get) _____

_____

9. Tommy went to the football game. (his father/let) _____

_____

10. The waiter cleared the table. (the busboy/help) _____

_____

L. Write a dialogue in which someone has just moved to your city. He/she wants to know about various services and where he/she can get jobs done. A partner answers the questions.

_____
_____
_____
_____
_____
_____
_____
_____
_____
_____
_____
_____
_____
_____
_____
_____

M. Write a composition about the following situation.

Imagine you or your friend bought an old, run-down house. Everything inside and outside needed to be fixed, washed, painted, cleared, replaced. Before you moved in, you had the house completely renovated. Using causative constructions, tell what changes you or your friend had made to the house.

_____
_____
_____
_____
_____
_____
_____

Unit XIX

Gerunds and Infinitives

A. Construct <u>where</u> questions with the verb <u>go</u>. Then answer your questions with a gerund. Use the cues provided. (Watch your verb tenses.)

Example: *dance – last night*
Where did you go last night?
I went dancing with my friend.

1. fish – last summer _____

_____

2. jog – this afternoon _____

_____

3. swim – now _____

_____

4. ski – this winter _____

_____

5. hike – next month _____

_____

6. shop – next Saturday _____

_____

7. canoe – last summer holiday _____

_____

8. camp – every August _____

_____

9. mountain climb – next June _____

_____

10. skate – before you came to class _____

_____

B. Combine each of the following pairs of sentences. Make one sentence using a gerund construction. Omit any unnecessary words.

Example: *The children wanted to have a picnic. They suggested it.*
The children suggested having a picnic.

1. They often play golf. They enjoy it._____

_____

2. I'll lend you my car. I don't mind. _____

_____

3. Mary works the night shift. She detests it._____

_____

4. He couldn't go skiing last weekend. He postponed it. _____

_____

5. Paul has painted his house. He's finished it. _____

_____

6. Steven broke up with his girlfriend. He regrets it. _____

_____

7. My sister was an avid snowboarder. She had an accident has quit._____

_____

8. When Miguel lived in Spain he went to the beach every day. He misses that. _____

_____

9. Tony used my car without asking for permission. He denies it. _____

_____

10. I'd like to buy a sail boat. I'm considering it. _____

_____

C. Complete the following sentences with a gerund phrase.
Example: I've just finished (reading a novel for my English class).

1. People from my country enjoy _____

2. Canadians often avoid _____

3. Since I'm planning to take a winter vacation, I'm considering _____

_____

4. I was tired so I quit_____

5. I regret _____during my childhood.

6. The weather was miserable, so we postponed _____

7. The burglar denied _____

8. If you keep_____you'll succeed.

9. I often think about my life before I came to Canada. I miss_____
_____; however, I don't miss _____

10. Do you ever object to _____ ?

11. You can only learn to speak well by _____

12. After_____I felt at home here.

13. Why do Canadians always talk about _____ ?

14. I never feel like _____

15. Canadian children are fond of _____

16. My mother is against _____

17. Are you proud of _____?

18. I often spend my time _____

19. My best friend is interested in_____

D. Fill in the blanks with a preposition and a gerund.

1. I plan _____ my children shopping this week.

2. We are interested _____ Canadian friends.

3. We're thinking _____ to Victoria for our summer vacation.

4. Are you excited _____ to the football game?

5. You don't like skiing because you are afraid _____ .

6. Sharon is engaged. She's looking forward _____ married.

7. Many people are fond _____ popcorn at the movies.

8. Do all restaurants insist _____ men _____ jackets and ties?

9. I apologize _____ not _____ on time.

10. Canadians often talk _____ .

11. Have you changed your mind _____ another course?

E. Rewrite the following paragraph. Change the underlined sections to gerund phrases. It may be necessary to add other information.

Mr. Gomez is happy about his life in Canada. He is used to work at a downtown bank and is good at his job. He looks forward to a raise next month. In his leisure time, Mr. Gomez enjoys football games and movies. In addition, he spends time at parties or sometimes feels like dinner with friends on weekends. He has never regretted that he came to Canada even though he has missed his old friends. This newcomer is accustomed to life in Canada.

Mr. Gomez is happy about living in Canada._____

_____

_____

_____

_____

_____

_____

_____

_____

_____

F. Answer the following questions in complete sentences using infinitive constructions.

1. What would you offer to do if an elderly lady were standing on a crowded bus and you were sitting? _____

2. What was the first thing you wanted to do when you arrived here? _____

_____

3. Name one thing you hope to do in the near future. _____

_____

4. Why did you decide to come here?_____

5. What is one thing people need to do if they want to make new friends? _____

_____

6. Name one thing you decided not to do after you moved here. _____

_____

7. If you became a Canadian citizen what would you promise to do? _____

_____

G. Think about someone you met when you first came here. Write two paragraphs telling some of the things this person told you in order to help you get used to living here. Use the following verb cues after first identifying the person who gave you advice.

1. What did he advise/urge/encourage/remind/teach/expect/ask you to do?

2. What did he tell/warn/persuade/instruct you not to do?

_____
_____
_____
_____
_____
_____
_____
_____
_____
_____
_____
_____
_____
_____
_____
_____
_____
_____
_____
_____
_____
_____
_____
_____

H. Fill in the blanks of the following paragraph with a suitable verb and any other necessary information. Be sure to use the correct form of the verb.

I hope _____ you something important about your new life in Canada. If you decide _____ here, I urge you _____ one of the official language. Don't pretend _____ when you don't understand. Instead, I encourage you _____ language classes as soon as possible. Your new surroundings will not seem _____ so strange after someone teaches you _____.

I. Complete the following sentences adding a gerund construction. Then, rewrite the sentence using an infinitive construction.

Example: *Next winter I might try ice fishing.*
   Next winter I might try to ice fish.

1. As soon as I arrived here, I began _____

_____

2. When I go out on weekends, I prefer _____

_____

3. On my days off, I can't stand _____

_____

4. Whenever I eat out, I like _____

_____

5. After I have lived here for a few years, I intend _____

_____

6. I hate _____ but I love _____ on weekends.

_____

7. After I finish this course, I might continue _____

_____

8. I always start _____ during funny movies.

_____

J. Write a complete sentence using the given cues and adding any necessary vocabulary. If the sentence has two possible forms, write them.

Example: *Jack – like – play – soccer – every Saturday afternoon.*
   Jack likes to play soccer every Saturday afternoon.
   Jack likes playing soccer every Saturday afternoon.

1. Sue – intend – stay – in this city – forever

_____

_____

2. We – not enjoy – go – rock concerts

_____

_____

3. You – avoid – drink too much – parties

_____

_____

4. My son – love – watch – hockey games – TV

_____

_____

5. Please, start – eat – without me. I – be late – tonight

_____

_____

6. Prefer – you – visit friends – stay home – tonight?

_____

_____

7. He – continue – attend – night school – next term

_____

_____

8. My uncle – stop – smoke – last month

_____

_____

9. I – can't stand – wait in line – bank

_____

_____

10. Plan – you – have – vacation – P.E.I. – next summer?

_____

_____

11. Renée – regret – not go – ski – last weekend

_____

_____

K. Read the given situations and then complete the sentence which follows.

1. Gail hasn't eaten dessert in four weeks. She's stopped _____

2. While walking down the street, I saw a newspaper stand. I wanted a newpaper so I stopped

_____

3. Yesterday was my mother's birthday. I sent her a card. I remembered _____

_____

4. Joe always goes to church on Sundays. He never forgets _____

5. Mary left her house in a hurry because she was late for work. She left the door open. She forgot _____

6. Lee had an argument with her boyfriend. They didn't see each other for a week. They stopped _____

7. Lam always enjoyed celebrating the new year in his country. He often thinks about those good times. He remembers _____

8. Anh used to go to the International Students' Club. He doesn't go any more. He has stopped

_____

9. I know it's important to leave a tip in a restaurant. I never forget _____

_____

10. Sue is angry with her boyfriend, Jack, because he didn't give her a valentine on Valentine's day. Poor Jack forgot _____

L. For each of the following, make a new sentence in which the subject changes to either a gerund or <u>it</u> + verb <u>to be</u> + adjective + infinitive.

Example: *Skiing is fun.*   or   *It's wise to lock your doors.*
             It's fun to ski.   *Locking your doors is wise.*

1. Shouting in public is rude. _____

2. It's important to line up for service in banks. _____

_____

3. Wearing warm winter clothes is necessary. _____

4. It's a good idea to exercise daily. _____

5. It's wrong to wear blue jeans to an interview. _____

_____

6. Smoking in class is unacceptable. _____

7. It is unhealthy to drink a lot of beer. _____

_____

8. Throwing garbage in the street is illegal. _____

_____

M. Write five sentences for each of the following.

In my country, I used to (e.g., ride a bicycle to work); now I have to get used to (e.g., taking three buses to work).

At first, I couldn't get used to (e.g., drinking coffee black), but now I'm getting used to (e.g., drinking coffee without milk).

_____
_____
_____
_____
_____
_____
_____
_____
_____
_____
_____
_____

_____

_____

_____

_____

_____

_____

_____

N. Fill in the blanks with a correct form of the verb given. If possible, provide alternative forms.

1. When you have finished (do) _____ your homework, let's go to a movie.

2. I prefer (play) _____ cards than board games.

3. We hope (learn) _____ how to refinish furniture at night school.

4. Tamara agreed (knit) _____ me a sweater for Christmas.

5. My friends and I like (square dance) _____ on weekends.

6. You forgot (find out) _____ what time the movie begins.

7. Jim avoids (do) _____ strenuous exercise. He has back problems.

8. I hate (exercise) _____ but I know it's good for me.

9. Did you enjoy (watch) _____ the Grey Cup on TV?

10. I regret (not learn) _____ to ski when I was young.

11. My mother would appreciate (hear) _____ from me once a week, but I'm so busy that it's difficult to write that often.

12. My uncle has decided (buy) _____ a large, color TV.

13. Try (talk) _____ to the manager about the poor service.

14. Would you like (sleep) _____ in a tent or a hotel room?

15. Please stop (speak) _____ so loudly.

16. We've just finished (watch) _____ our favorite program.

17. Would you mind (turn) _____ the music down, please?

18. I can't stand (wait) _____ in line.

19. Don't forget (call) _____ Jean if you can't go to her party.

20. Will you consider (take) _____ a camping trip in the Rockies this summer?

21. Do you deny (eat) _____ a piece of cake before supper?

22. I'll never get used to (drink) _____ milk. I just don't like it.

23. Because of the rainy weather, we'll postpone (camp) _____ in the national park until it is warmer.

24. I forgot (reserve) _____ a ticket for the play. Now it's too late. It has been sold out!

25. When I was a child I used to (roller skate) _____ .

O. Write a composition about living in Canada indicating both the good and the bad points. Using gerunds and infinitives, tell about your feelings, your hopes and plans for the future.

_____

_____

_____

_____

_____

_____

_____

_____

_____

_____

_____

_____

_____

_____

_____

_____

_____

_____

_____

_____

_____

_____

_____

_____

_____

_____

_____

_____

_____

_____

_____

_____

_____

_____

_____

_____

_____

_____

Unit XX

Reported Speech

A. Change the following sentences from direct into reported speech.

Example: He said, "I want to make a local call."
He said (that) he wanted to make a local call.

1. My friend said, "I'll use the public phone at the corner." _____

_____

2. Linda said, "I don't have any change for this phone." _____

_____

3. He remarked, "There's no dial tone, so I'll have to use another phone." _____

_____

4. I said, "The phone has been ringing for at least two minutes." _____

_____

5. The operator said to me, "You won't get your coins back if someone answers the phone."

_____

6. Georgio said, "Since it's my mother's birthday tomorrow, I'm going to call her long
distance." _____

_____

7. My friend said, "I can't understand what the operator is saying." _____

_____

8. The operator said, "I can try your call again later." _____

_____

9. Antonio said to me, "It is cheaper to call your family after midnight." _____

_____

10. Mother said, "We should rent a push-button phone." _____

_____

11. I said to my room-mate, "You have to tell the phone company to disconnect our phone
before we move." _____

_____

12. The recording always says, "Please hang up and try your call again." _____

_____

13. He said to me, "You ought to direct dial because it's cheaper." _____

_____

14. Jim stated, "I'll try this number again tomorrow." _____

_____

15. My sister said, "I want the operator to connect my call." _____

16. Marian said, "I don't know my brother's area code in Halifax." _____

17. I said to the operator, "I am calling person-to-person now because I want to speak only to my son."_____

18. The operator said to me, "You can't use direct dial service anywhere else in the world." _____

19. She said, "I've always called collect because my father doesn't mind paying the bill." _____

20. The operator said to me, "You will be billed separately for this long distance call." _____

B. Change the following direct speech into reported questions.

Example: I asked, "Can I send a telegram at any time of day?"
I asked if I could send a telegram at any time of day.

1. Tony asked me, "How long does it take for an e-mail to reach Italy?"_____

2. The stranger asked, "Where is the nearest Post Office?" _____

3. Mary asked me, "Are you going to send a money order?" _____

4. I asked you, "Have you ever sent money to your parents by telegram?"_____

5. I asked the clerk, "Do you have a form which I can write a message on?" _____

6. He asked me, "When do you want your family to receive this message?"_____

7. She said to him, "Did you include a self-addressed, stamped envelope for a reply?" _____

8. I asked her, "Did you get a receipt after you had paid for the fax?"_____

9. He said to me, "Were you talking to the operator a minute ago?"_____

10. I asked the phone company, "How much does it cost to install a phone in my apartment?" _____

11. She asked her son, "Why do you want cable TV?"_____

12. Someone asked me, "Do you have a CD player?" _____

13. The teacher asked them, "Did you have a TV in your country?" _____

14. I asked my room-mate, "How many channels can we get?" _____

15. Juan asked her, "Are you going to watch the movie at my place tonight?" _____

16. I was asked, "Which television commercial do you enjoy the most?" _____

17. I asked the clerk, "Where should I take my radio for repair?" _____

18. You asked us, "Do you ever listen to classical music on the radio?" _____

19. I asked her, "Have you just recorded a message to send to your family?" _____

20. She asked me, "Must I pay my telephone bill at the end of this month?" _____

C. Change the following direct commands into reported speech.

Example: John said to me, "Call me after midnight."
John told me to call him after midnight.

1. The announcer said to the viewers, "Don't adjust your TV set." _____

2. The operator said to me, "Deposit ninety cents in the call box." _____

3. I urged my husband, "Please buy a clock radio for our bedroom." _____

4. She said to the child, "Be polite when you answer the phone." _____

5. She said to me, "Never tell the caller your name." _____

6. The recording said, "Please leave your name and number at the sound of the beep."

7. I encouraged Jack, "Don't rent a phone because it's cheaper in the long run to buy one."

8. The operator told us, "Hang up and dial again." _____

9. My son said to me, "Don't deposit any money if you are calling the operator." _____

10. She said to him, "Don't call me again at this hour." _____

11. "Call me after work," he told me. _____

12. My father said to me, "Listen to the weather forecast on Channel 1." _____

13. The clerk said to me, "Pay your bill or we will disconnect your phone." _____

14. The newscaster said, "Do not go out because the road conditions are treacherous." _____

15. He said to me angrily, "Don't do that again!" _____

D. Change the following statements into noun clauses to complete the sentences.

Example: *"Why are you sending a fax?" I was angry when he asked me why I was sending a fax.*

1. "You should read the grocery ads in the Thursday paper." She told me _____

2. "Did you read the headlines in tonight's paper?" The teacher asked me _____

3. "Where did you get your information?" I didn't want to answer when he asked me _____

4. "Look at the hilarious comic strip." My husband was laughing when he told me _____

5. "I never look at the sports section in the newspaper." He stated that _____

6. "Are there commercials on TV in your country?" During our conversation he asked me _____

7. "My children can't watch this program because it is violent." I told the babysitter _____

8. "Are color monitors more expensive than black and white?" We asked the salesperson _____

9. "Don't watch this program because you won't like it." My mother told me _____

10. "Who decides which program to watch in your house?" I asked my neighbor _____

11. "What kinds of programs are on radio in your country?" While we were talking, I asked him

12. "Please buy a TV with a remote control." I wanted to tell him _____

_____

13. "Will my English improve if I watch TV?" You asked your teacher _____

_____

14. "There's going to be a music special on CBC tomorrow night." When I saw my uncle I told

him _____

E. Complete the following sentences.

1. I wonder if _____

2. The announcer said _____

3. My friend urged me _____

4. The operator repeated _____

5. The caller stated that _____

6. My sister told me _____

7. You asked me _____

8. The man reported _____

9. The editor commented _____

10. Joe asked why _____

F. Fill in the blanks of the following sentences using the correct form of say or tell.

1. She _____ me to call a television repairman because the TV was out of
order.

2. Mary _____ that she had called the telephone company business office to
ask about her bill.

3. Please _____ us why you enjoy that program so much.

4. Don't _____ me to buy a home computer; I can't afford one.

5. He _____ that he was looking for the number in the phone book.

6. You _____ your children to be quiet when you are on the phone.

7. The operator _____ that the number was out of service.

8. We _____ the repair clerk to check the problem with our phone.

9. You _____ her that you needed directory assistance.

10. The telephone company always _____ you if your account is overdue.

G. Change the following dialogue into reported speech. Vary your use of introductory words.

Kim: *I want to call 214-555-5665 please.*

Operator: *Who are you calling?*

Kim: *I'm calling Mr. Lan Nguyen.*

Operator: *What kind of call would you like to make?*

Kim:	It will be a person-to-person call.
Operator:	Don't dial. I'll call the number for you. Please deposit $1.50.
Kim:	Are you trying now?
Operator:	Yes, I am. Your number is ringing.
Kim:	I can hear it.
Operator:	Go ahead. Mr. Nguyen is on the line. After three minutes I will remind you to finish your conversation or deposit more money.
Kim:	Thank you, Operator. Goodbye.

H. Choose a comic strip with dialogue, an advertisement or a question and answer article (e.g., Ann Landers) from a newspaper or magazine. Summarize your clipping by using reported speech. Include the article with your paragraph.

I. Tape a segment of the news or sports from the radio. Summarize, using reported speech. Include the tape with your summary.

_____
_____
_____
_____
_____
_____
_____
_____
_____
_____
_____
_____
_____
_____

J. Interview two or three classmates about their attitudes toward television. Take notes, then write three or more paragraphs in reported speech to tell of your interview. Choose from the suggestions below and any other ideas you may have.

1. Do you watch TV? When? Where? How often? What kind of shows?

2. Tell about your favorite program. What kinds of programs do you dislike?

3. Do you like commercials? If so, which ones? Explain why or why not.

4. Did you have a TV before you came to Canada? Describe television programming in your country.

_____
_____
_____
_____
_____
_____
_____
_____
_____
_____
_____
_____
_____
_____

Vocabulary
Unit II

bank draft _____

bond _____

borrow _____

budget (v., n.) _____

consumer loan _____

credit union _____

endorse _____

foreclosure _____

interest (rate of) _____

invest _____

lend _____

mortgage _____

overdraft _____

savings/chequing account _____

transfer _____

trust company _____

utility bill _____

withdrawal/deposit slip _____

_____

_____

_____

_____

_____

_____

_____

_____

_____

_____

_____

_____

_____

_____

_____

_____

_____

Unit III

ache _____

balanced diet _____

Canada Food Guide _____

dose _____

food group_____

menu _____

nutrients_____

nutrition/nutritionist_____

pharmacy _____

prescription _____

reservation_____

specialize _____

tip _____

vitamins _____

_____

_____

_____

_____

_____

_____

_____

_____

_____

_____

_____

_____

_____

_____

_____

_____

_____

_____

_____

_____

_____

_____

_____

_____

Unit IV

allergy _____

antibiotics _____

antihistamine _____

be (feel) well (sick) _____

contagious _____

crutch _____

dental work _____

diet aid _____

emergency _____

family doctor (physician, specialist) _____

fever _____

first aid _____

have a temperature _____

have (get) a check-up _____

headache _____

immunization _____

medical history _____

mouthwash _____

operation _____

over-the-counter drugs _____

pale _____

patient _____

pill/capsule _____

rash _____

remedy (cure) _____

sore throat _____

stomach ache _____

surgery _____

symptom _____

transfusion _____

vaporizer _____

well-baby clinic _____

X-ray (v), X-ray (n,) _____

_____

_____

Unit V

boil _____

brunch _____

can you come _____

celebrate _____

come over (drop by) and see me_____

do the dishes _____

drop in (drop by) _____

formal _____

give (someone) a lift (ride) _____

informal _____

kettle _____

punctual _____

see you (later, at 6:00, on Monday)_____

set the table _____

thanks for (dinner; having me, us)_____

_____

_____

_____

_____

_____

_____

_____

_____

_____

_____

_____

_____

_____

_____

_____

_____

_____

_____

_____

_____

_____

_____

_____

Unit VI

adolescence _____

career _____

child-raising _____

companionship _____

down jacket _____

dry clean _____

extended family _____

family ties _____

generation _____

gloves (mittens) _____

independence _____

lifestyle _____

nuclear family (immediate family) _____

partner _____

peer _____

puberty _____

retirement community _____

scarf _____

senior citizen _____

try on _____

_____

_____

_____

_____

_____

_____

_____

_____

_____

_____

_____

_____

_____

_____

_____

_____

Unit VII

author _____

biography _____

bookmobile _____

branch _____

call number _____

call slip _____

catalogue_____

check out (a book) _____

due date _____

encyclopedia_____

fine (n.) _____

librarian _____

look up (a book, card)_____

non-fiction _____

novel _____

overdue _____

periodical _____

photocopier_____

reference_____

_____

_____

_____

_____

_____

_____

_____

_____

_____

_____

_____

_____

_____

_____

_____

_____

_____

_____

Unit VIII

change (n.) _____

change of address card _____

customs declaration form _____

deliver _____

enclose _____

mailbox _____

money order _____

parcel, package _____

post office box_____

redirect _____

registered letter_____

return address _____

seal _____

special delivery _____

stick (v.)_____

surface mail _____

telegram _____

_____

_____

_____

_____

_____

_____

_____

_____

_____

_____

_____

_____

_____

_____

_____

_____

_____

_____

Unit IX

apprentice (n., v.) _____

assignment _____

compulsory _____

drop out (n., v.) _____

elementary school (primary school) _____

enrol _____

expel _____

further education _____

graduate (from) _____

high school (secondary school) _____

installments _____

junior high school _____

kindergarten _____

pay attention to _____

physical education _____

prerequisite _____

register _____

skip (school, i.e., play truant, play hookey) _____

   (a class, a grade) _____

technical school _____

TOEFL _____

transcript _____

transfer _____

vocational school _____

_____

_____

_____

_____

_____

_____

_____

_____

_____

_____

_____

Unit X

appliances _____

asking price _____

damage deposit _____

down payment _____

eviction _____

existing mortgage _____

expire _____

landlord _____

laundry facilities _____

lease (n.) _____

legal fees _____

list (v.) (a house, apartment) _____

offer to purchase _____

open house _____

possession date _____

property tax _____

rent controls _____

replace _____

tenant _____

vacant _____

_____

_____

_____

_____

_____

_____

_____

_____

_____

_____

_____

_____

_____

_____

_____

Unit XI

blood pressure _____

break into _____

credentials _____

engine trouble _____

faint (v.) _____

flag down _____

hazard lights _____

hazardous _____

intercom _____

page (v.) _____

Poison Control Centre _____

single car accident _____

siren _____

skid _____

strenuous _____

stretcher _____

tow truck _____

wheelchair _____

_____
_____
_____
_____
_____
_____
_____
_____
_____
_____
_____
_____
_____
_____
_____
_____
_____
_____
_____
_____
_____

Unit XII

automatic/standard transmission _____

bargain (n.), bargain for (v.) _____

bill of sale _____

boost _____

compact/luxury car _____

expire _____

impaired driving _____

jack (n.) _____

permanent/temporary license _____

registration _____

renew _____

road test _____

self service _____

tune up _____

valid _____

_____

_____

_____

_____

_____

_____

_____

_____

_____

_____

_____

_____

_____

_____

_____

_____

_____

_____

_____

_____

_____

_____

Unit XIII

argue a case _____

breathalyzer test _____

commissioner _____

commit a crime _____

court _____

discrimination _____

file a complaint _____

fine (n., v.) _____

hire _____

Human Rights Commission _____

inherit _____

Landlord and Tenant Advisory Board _____

Legal Aid _____

Office of Vital Statistics _____

petition (n.) _____

summons _____

testimony _____

trial _____

will (n.) _____

witness _____

_____

_____

_____

_____

_____

_____

_____

_____

_____

_____

_____

_____

_____

_____

_____

_____

_____

_____

Unit XIV

assessment _____

deadline _____

deduct _____

deduction _____

file a return _____

incorporate _____

installments _____

overpaid _____

penalty _____

property tax _____

refund (n., v.) _____

Revenue Canada _____

T-4 slip _____

tax bracket _____

tax clinic _____

workers' compensation _____

_____

_____

_____

_____

_____

_____

_____

_____

_____

_____

_____

_____

_____

_____

_____

_____

_____

Unit XV

baggage claim _____

bus pass _____

cancellation insurance _____

carry-on case _____

customs _____

customs inspector _____

direct flight _____

express bus _____

guest house _____

hitch hike _____

luxury liner _____

non-stop flight _____

round trip _____

schedule _____

souvenir _____

stop-over (n.) _____

talkative _____

_____

_____

_____

_____

_____

_____

_____

_____

_____

_____

_____

_____

_____

_____

_____

_____

_____

_____

_____

_____

_____

Unit XVI

apprentice (n., v.) _____

colleague _____

confidence _____

cover letter _____

experience (n.) _____

expand _____

fire (v.) _____

hire _____

interview (n., v.) _____

job opening _____

job opportunities _____

letter of application _____

minimum wage _____

personal data _____

progressive _____

prospective employer _____

qualifications _____

quit _____

reference _____

résumé _____

skill _____

top-notch _____

unemployment insurance _____

_____

_____

_____

_____

_____

_____

_____

_____

_____

_____

_____

_____

Unit XVII

appoint _____

B.N.A. Act _____

ballot _____

bill (n.) _____

cabinet _____

campaign (n., v.) _____

candidate _____

Charter of Rights _____

constituency _____

Constitution _____

debate (n., v.) _____

document _____

elect _____

elegible _____

enumerator _____

House of Commons _____

issue (n.) _____

Member of Parliament (M.P.) _____

opposition _____

polls _____

policy _____

protest march _____

represent _____

representative _____

rights _____

security risk _____

Senate _____

submit _____

_____

_____

_____

_____

_____

_____

_____

_____

Unit XVIII

be out of order _____

fertilize _____

fix (a TV, the roof, etc.) _____

gas meter _____

install_____

mow the lawn_____

perm (n., v.) _____

weeds _____

wrinkled _____

_____

_____

_____

_____

_____

_____

_____

_____

_____

_____

_____

_____

_____

_____

_____

_____

_____

_____

_____

_____

_____

_____

_____

_____

_____

_____

Unit XIX

avid _____

be on time _____

can't stand (to do/doing something) _____

cause (v.) _____

consider _____

delay _____

encourage _____

insist (on) _____

keep (on) _____

neglect _____

persuade _____

postpone _____

remind _____

rude _____

urge (v.) _____

_____

_____

_____

_____

_____

_____

_____

_____

_____

_____

_____

_____

_____

_____

_____

_____

_____

_____

_____

_____

_____

_____

_____

Unit XX

area code _____

be off the hook _____

be out of service (out of order) _____

call collect _____

comment (v.)_____

deposit (v.) _____

dial tone _____

direct dial _____

disconnect_____

hang up _____

observe_____

person-to-person _____

phone booth _____

pre-pay _____

remote control _____

request (v.) _____

slot (n.)_____

state (v.) _____

station-to-station _____

treacherous_____

unlisted _____

_____

_____

_____

_____

_____

_____

_____

_____

_____

_____

_____

_____

_____

_____

_____

_____